THE UNNATURAL ENEMY

THE UNNATURAL ENEMY

ESSAYS ON HUNTING

Vance Bourjaily.

FOREWORD BY EDWARD ABBEY
ILLUSTRATIONS BY DAVID LEVINE

The University of Arizona Press
TUCSON, ARIZONA

About the Author

VANCE BOURJAILY is a novelist and essayist whose work has appeared in many national publications. Among his books are *Now Playing at Canterbury, The End of My Life, Country Matters,* and *A Game Men Play.* Bourjaily teaches fiction writing at the University of Arizona.

THE UNIVERSITY OF ARIZONA PRESS

First Printing 1984
Manufactured in the U.S.A.

"The Goose Pits" and "The Unnatural Enemy" originally appeared in *The New Yorker.* An episode from "Opening Days" originally appeared in *Esquire,* under the title "One Hell of a Duck Hunt." Copyright © by Esquire, Inc., 1963.

Library of Congress Cataloging in Publication Data

Bourjaily, Vance Nye.
The unnatural enemy.

1. Hunting. 2. Fowling. I. Title.
SK33.B688   1984   799.2   84-8640
ISBN 0-8165-0884-4

CONTENTS

Foreword by Edward Abbey vii

Note: In which a Precedent is Elected but

Will Not Serve 1

1. How the Hours are Counted 5

2. Opening Days 29

3. The Goose Pits 67

4. In Fields Near Home 93

5. The Unnatural Enemy 135

6. Warm Again 152

FOREWORD

This is a book about hunting, and how can I write about that? Hunting is one of the hardest things even to think about. Such a storm of conflicting emotions!

I was born, bred, and raised on a farm in the Allegheny Mountains of Pennsylvania. A little sidehill farm in hardscrabble country, a land of marginal general farms, of submarginal specialized farms —our specialty was finding enough to eat without the shame of going on "The Relief," as we called it during the Great Depression of the 1930s. We lived in the hills, surrounded by scrubby third-growth forests, little coal-mining towns down in the valleys, and sulfur-colored creeks meandering among the corn patches. Few people could make a living from farming, alone: my father, for example, supplemented what little we produced on the farm by occasional work in the mines, by driving a school bus, by a one-man logging business, by peddling subscriptions to a farmer's magazine, and by attending every private and public shooting match within fifty miles of home—he was an expert small-bore rifleman and a member, for several years running, of the Pennsylvania state rifle team; he still has a sashful of medals to show for those years. He almost always brought back from the matches a couple of chickens, sometimes a turkey, once a yearling pig.

None of this was quite enough, all together, to keep a family of seven in meat, all the time, through the frozen Appalachian winters. So he hunted. We all hunted. All of our neighbors hunted. Nearly every boy I knew had his own rifle, and maybe a shotgun too, by the time he was twelve years old.

What did we hunt? Cottontail rabbit, first and foremost; we'd kill them, clean them, skin them, cut them up; my mother deep-fried them in bread crumbs and cooked and canned the surplus in Mason jars, as she did tomatoes, stringbeans, succotash, pork sausage, peaches, pears, sweet corn, everything else that would keep. We had no deep-freeze; in fact, we had no electricity until the Rural Electrification Administration reached our neck of the woods in 1940.

So rabbit was almost a staple of our diet, as good and familiar to us as chicken. Fence-row chicken, we called it. My father seldom bothered with squirrel, but my brothers and I potted a few with our little Sears & Roebuck single-shot .22s, out among the great ancient white oaks and red oaks that were still standing in our woodlot. Squirrel meat can be good, but not so good as rabbit, and a squirrel is much harder to kill; we missed about ten for every one we hit.

There were no wild ducks or other waterfowl in the hills; our only gamebird was the ringneck pheasant, rising with a thrilling rush from the corn stubble. My father bagged a few of those with his old taped-together double-barrel shotgun. Not many. He didn't like to hunt with a shotgun. Wasteful, he thought, and the shells were too expensive, and besides, he disliked chewing on lead pellets. The shotgun was primarily a weapon (though never needed) for home defense. Most of the time he shot rabbits with his target rifle, a massive magazine-loaded .22 with a peep-sight. Shot them sitting.

Was that legal? Probably not. I don't remember. But he had a good eye. And he was a hunter—not a sportsman. He hunted for one purpose only: to put meat on the table.

We kept a couple of beagle hounds on the place, but their job was to lie under the front porch and bark at strangers. Only when our Uncle Jack came out from town, with his sleek gleaming 16-gauge pumpgun (as we called it), and the red bandana and hunting license pinned to the back of his hunting coat, only then would our old man load his own shotgun and turn loose the dogs for some conventional-style sport hunting through the fields and along the edge of the woods. What my father really liked about those occasions was not the shooting but the talk, the wild stories—Uncle Jack was a great storyteller—and the "male bonding."

And then there were the deer. The woods of Pennsylvania swarmed with deer, though not as many then as now, when so many small old farms, abandoned, have gone back to brush, thicket, trees. There were even a few black bears still wandering the woods, rarely seen. But deer was the principal game.

My father usually bought a license for deer, when he could afford it, but only because the penalty for getting caught with an untagged deer would have been a small financial catastrophe.

In any case, with or without a license, he always killed his deer on the evening before opening day, while those red-coated fellows from the towns and cities were busy setting up their elaborate camps along the back roads, stirring the deer into movement. He was not a stickler for strict legality, and he believed, as most country men did, that fear tainted the meat and that therefore it was better to get your deer before the chase, the gunnery—The Terror—began. We liked our venison poached. (As a result I find that after these many years I retain more admiration and respect for the honest serious poacher than I do or ever could for the so-called "gentleman hunter.")

My old man practiced what we called "still hunting." On the day before opening, about noon, when the deer were bedded down for their midday siesta, he'd go out with his gun, his cornfodder-tan canvas coat with its many big pockets, and his coal-miner's oval-shaped lunch bucket full of hot coffee and sandwiches and Mother's stewed-raisin cookies, and he'd pick a familiar spot along one of the half-dozen familiar game paths in our neighborhood, settle down in the brush with his back to a comfortable tree, and wait. And keep on waiting, sometimes into the long autumn twilight, until at last the first somewhat nervous, always uneasy deer appeared. Doe or buck, he always shot whatever came first. You can't eat antlers, for Christ's sake!

Usually he shot his deer with a "punkin ball" from the battered, dangerous, taped-up shotgun. But at least once, as I recall, he dropped a doe with his target rifle, like a rabbit. Drilled her right between the eyes with a neat little .22-caliber long-rifle bullet. Those deer slugs for the shotgun were expensive.

Then he'd drag the deer into the brush, out of sight, and wait some more, to see if anyone had noticed the shot. When nothing happened, he hung the deer to the nearest tree limb, dressed it out, and ate the liver for supper. If it was a legal kill he would wait through the night, tag it, and take it home by car first thing in the morning. If not, he slung the carcass over his shoulders and toted it home through the woods and over the hills in the dark. He was a strong, large, and resolute sort of man then, back in the Thirties and early Forties. Nowadays, getting on a bit—he was born in 1901—he is still oversize, for an old man, but not so strong physically. Nor so resolute. He works four or five hours a day, alone, out in the woods, cutting down trees, and then quits. He gave up deer hunting long ago, more than thirty years ago.

Why? "Well," he explains, "we don't need the meat anymore." Now that was how my brothers and I learned about hunting. They still like to go out for deer now and then, but it's road hunting, with good companions, not "still hunting." I wonder if anybody hunts in that fashion these days. I did a lot of deer hunting in New Mexico from 1947 through the 1950s, during my student years and later, when I was living on seasonal jobs with the Park Service and Forest Service, often married, trying to write books. As my father had taught me, I usually went out on the day before opening. Much safer then, for one thing, before those orange-vested hordes were turned loose all over the landscape, shooting at everything that moved.

Gradually, from year to year, my interest in hunting, as a sport, waned away to nothing. I began to realize that what I liked best about hunting was the companionship of a few good old trusted male buddies in the out-of-doors. Anything, any excuse, to get out into the hills, away from the crowds, to live, if only for a few days, beyond the wall. That was the point of it.

So why lug a ten-pound gun along? I began leaving my rifle in the truck. Then I left it at home. The last time I looked down the bore of that old piece there was a little spider living down there.

"We don't need the meat anymore," says my old man. And I say, let the mountain lions have those deer; they need the meat more than I do. Let the Indians have it, or hungry college students or unpublished writers, or anyone else trying to get by on welfare, food stamps, and hope. When the money began arriving from New York by airmail, those checks with my name on them, like manna from Heaven, I gave up hunting deer. I had no need. Every time you eat a cow, I tell myself, you are saving the life of an elk, or two muledeer, or about two dozen javelina. Let those wild creatures live. Let being be, said Martin Heidegger. Of course, they're going to perish anyway, I know, whether by lion or wolf or starvation or disease—but so are we. We are all going to perish, and most of us miserably, by war or in a hospital, unless we are very lucky. Or very resolute. I am aware of that fact and of our fate, and furthermore, I have no objections to it, none whatsoever. I fear pain, suffering, the likely humiliations of old age (unless I am lucky or resolute), but I do not fear death. Death is simply and obviously a part of the process;

the old, sooner or later, have got to get out of the way and make room for the young.

The subject remains: death. Blood sport. The instinct to hunt. The desire to kill. In the honest, engaging book that follows, Vance Bourjaily points out that Henry David Thoreau, notorious nature lover, was also a hunter and fisherman, on occasion. Indeed he was. And among the many things that Thoreau wrote on the matter was this, from *Walden:*

> There is a period in the history of the individual, as of the race, when the hunters are the "best men," as the Algonquins called them. We cannot but pity the boy who has never fired a gun; he is no more humane, while his education has been sadly neglected.

But he adds:

> No humane being, past the thoughtless age of boyhood, will wantonly murder any creature which holds its life by the same tenure he does. The hare in its extremity cries like a child. I warn you, mothers, that my sympathies do not make the usual *philanthropic* distinctions.

Thoreau concludes:

> But I see that if I were to live in a wilderness, I should become... a fisher and hunter in earnest.

In earnest. There lies the key to the ethical issue. That sly sophist Ortega y Gasset wrote, somewhere, that "one kills in order to have hunted." Not good enough. Thoreau would say, one kills in order to eat. The killing is justified by the need and must be done in a spirit of respect, reverence, gratitude. Otherwise hunting sinks to the level of mere sport, fun, "harvesting animals," *divertissement,* sadism.

Where did the ugly term "harvesting" come from? To speak of "harvesting" other living creatures, whether deer or elk or birds or cottontail rabbits, as if they were no more than a crop, exposes the meanest, cruelest, most narrow and homocentric of possible human attitudes toward the life that surrounds us. The word reveals the pervasive influence of utilitarian economics in the modern mindset; and of all the sciences, economics is the most crude, obtuse as well as dismal. Such doctrine insults and violates both humanity and life; and humanity will be, already is, the victim of it.

Now I have railed against the sportsman-hunter long enough. I wished only to explain why first my father and then I have given

[xi]

up hunting, for the time being. When times get hard again, as they surely will, when my family and kin need meat on the table, I shall not hesitate to take that old carbine down from the wall and ramrod that spider out of the barrel and wander back once more into the hills.

The Unnatural Enemy (man) deals mostly with bird and duck shooting, a sport of which I know nothing. But it is a branch of hunting and therefore what I have written here about hunting in general is not irrelevant. Vance Bourjaily touches on the questions I have raised, sometimes directly, sometimes by implication. He is fully aware of the moral concerns that the art of hunting arouses in our time, but he has resolved them differently. More power to him. He is a thoughtful, intelligent man and a first-rate American writer, and *The Unnatural Enemy* is a good book about the most ancient, primordial, and basic of human endeavors. I am pleased that the book is hereby revived and reissued, for it is worthy of consideration by all readers who enjoy a good story well told, whether they give a hoot in hell about hunting or not. I trust that most of its readers will hurry through my preliminary torments and get directly into the action. Cut through the barbed wire and get into the field. That's where the pleasure is, the thrill of the hunt!

"Paw," says my little brother, as the old man loads the shotgun, "let me shoot the deer this time."

"You shut up," I say.

Our father smiles. "Quiet," he whispers, "both of you. Maybe next year." He peers down the dim path in the woods, into the gathering evening. "Be real still now. They're a-comin'. And Ned—" He squeezes my shoulder. "You hold that light on 'em good and steady this time."

"Yes, sir," I whisper back. "Sure will, Paw."

EDWARD ABBEY

THE UNNATURAL ENEMY

Note: In which a Precedent is Elected but Will Not Serve

THERE IS A TRADITION I SHOULD LIKE TO FOLLOW, which is to open a sporting book with a dialogue in which the characters have Latin names. PISCATOR and AUCEPS and others are chatting along, in rather flowery sentences, arguing about sport. But I can recall this only out of affection, and even in setting out must make my first break with the tradition—and afterwards will find myself unable to follow any of the rest of it. The first break is this: that I can't really address another hunter in the dialogue, and give my voice the title which would make me spokesman. He is likely to be more VENATOR than I. I shall never break 25 clay birds in a row, or shoot a limit of mourning doves, and he may do both consistently. So I shall have to make him Reader, and myself Writer, and there goes tradition, right there.

LECTOR: Okay, Buster, what kind of book is this?

SCRIPTOR: I don't know. If it's any good, it's a kind of book that never was before.

LECTOR: Calm down. You can say what it's about, can't you?

[1]

SCRIPTOR: Yes. It's about hunting birds. Walking in fields. Messing around in boats. Going out sometimes with other men who hunt birds, walk fields, mess around in boats. It's about how the hours are counted.

LECTOR: The first chapter, you mean? Or the whole damn book?

SCRIPTOR: Well, the whole book, in a way.

LECTOR: What's it mean, how the hours are counted?

SCRIPTOR: Don't crowd me.

LECTOR: You'll come to that?

SCRIPTOR: Yes.

LECTOR: Mind saying when?

SCRIPTOR: In about 26 pages at the end of Chapter I. After I've discussed some books this one isn't like, and the men who wrote them.

LECTOR: Oh, boy, I can hardly wait. What do you want to get into stuff like that for?

SCRIPTOR: Self-indulgence, probably. Writing is my occupation; hunting is a preoccupation. The two so often conflict that it interests me when they occur together.

LECTOR: But there're hundreds of books you could talk about!

SCRIPTOR: I've picked just five. Particular books from which I imagined I might find out why I hunt. Or what sort of man to be, as a hunter. Something like that. And one of the five is a book that was never written.

LECTOR: That one must have done you a lot of good.

SCRIPTOR: It did, as a matter of fact. It gave me a book to try to imagine, and that helped me write this one. The man who never wrote it was called Nathanael West.

LECTOR: Sure, fine, look: when I'm in a marsh, and I have to, I'll pull my feet in and out and labor through the mud. But if there's a way around, I'll take it. Couldn't I just skip your 26 pages about other writers, and get to the hunting?

SCRIPTOR: I wish you would, if you feel that way about it. Skip from here to the last three paragraphs of the first chapter and you'll find the solution to the small riddle I've chosen to make of my chapter heading, about the hours. And after that the other chapters are all hunting stories. No more books mentioned until the last. But you may as well know the names of the other four writers who hunted birds, whom I'm going to write about: they were Edward, Duke of York. Henry Thoreau. Ivan Turgenev. And Ernest Hemingway.

LECTOR: And of course this fellow West. What was he? Big man with a gun?

SCRIPTOR: No. No, I don't think so.

LEARNING TO HUNT

1. How The Hours Are Counted

EDWARD, THE SECOND DUKE OF YORK, DID HIS BIRD hunting with falcons and flushing dogs, or sometimes with a net, slipping up within netting range of birds held by one of the original pointing dogs. They were called spaniels, because they came from Spain; this was just before and after 1400.

Edward is fascinating to a literary man. He seems to have been a straightforward, well-mannered, and agreeable enough Duke in real life, judging from his own writings. But Shakespeare, reading about him in Holinshed's Chronicles a couple of hundred years later, turned him into a double-dealing villain called Aumerle in the history play *Richard II*. Edward was Duke of Aumerle as a young man, until his father died and left the York title for him; Edward, as Aumerle, was loyal to the king who got deposed, which is why Shakespeare nailed him. This is the kind of penalty even a hunter has to pay for being on the losing side in a civil war. Some bourgeois playwright comes along who doesn't know a spaniel from a goshawk.

While he was exiled in France, the real-life Edward became friends, so historians guess, with a French nobleman named Gaston de Foix, who had written the first great book on hunting in the Christian era, a work called *La Chasse*. Later, imprisoned, Edward translated Gaston's book, adding five chapters of his own and making a number of changes—this is the only part of Edward's life to which my imagination will let me feel at all close. I know, if at long remove and great reduction, what it must have been like to stare out the high windows of Pevensey Castle, at the fine weather with the meadow grasses stirring in the sunshine and the floor of the forest dappled like a fawn's hide, horses grazing, dogs noisy in the kennels, herons in flight over the marsh—stare at it, remembering the cut of air and stroke of sun on free limbs, and sigh, and go back to writing the book. Well. Beats yearning, anyway, something to pass the long days while seasons change—political seasons for the Duke, along with natural; regulatory seasons for me.

But it is only as another writer that I have much sense that I know what life was like (at times) for Edward. As hunters we do totally different things, for almost totally different reasons. In *The Master of Game*, which is what he called his adaptation of Gaston's book, Edward is concerned mostly with riding after stags, wolves, boar, and foxes, and with coursing hares. Bird hunting even then had a natural restriction: the hawks were only fit to fly six months of the year, peculiar things happening to their feathers the rest of the time. Even the spaniels were only a recreational novelty, time out from the serious matter of riding down a stag, dismounting, and killing him with your sword. When one thinks of the way they made their kills, it must have been more like bullfighting than it is like our own hunting.

Their kind of hunting had, of course, two kinds of motive which ours lacks: it provided constant exercise of military weapons and techniques at a time when leading armies was a duke's chief responsibility (and Edward, it should be said, died a soldier's death, not a traitor's, leading the English vanguard at the great battle of Agincourt). And hunting was also still important economically, as a source of food. Finally, hunting was a great ceremony, in a ceremonial age, and though there is a survival of this aspect of the Duke's kind of chase in fox hunting on horseback, it doesn't attract me much. As for falconry, in which at least the game pursued is the same as that with which I am engaged, I shall have to describe what little I have seen of hawks and hawking to show why I feel no sense of spiritual inheritance from Duke Edward even here. It happened, not long ago, that I met a falconer.

The falconer is a strange, rather nice man, with a master's degree in philosophy and a fascination for those things in nature which are deadly—he has handled rattlesnakes and kept piranhas in his goldfish bowl. And he has trained and flown one of almost every kind in the great chain of killer birds. But his personal identification is not so much with renaissance or medieval England, and the Age of Chivalry, as with the ancient, magic-riddled worlds of Egypt and Persia, where falconry began.

The first time I visited him he was living in a small suburban house, with his wife and four children, on the outskirts of a Southern industrial city, working as a claims adjuster. There was a swingset in the yard, as in most neighboring yards, and a sandbox beside which was a homemade cage consisting of a large crate, set on a rough table, with chicken wire across the open front.

We chatted for a few minutes in the house; then Zerbe offered to show me the falcons. As I preceded him out the door, I turned towards the chickenwire cage.

"Not that way," he said.

"They're not in the cage?"

He laughed, and led me to the garage. It was gloomy inside, but I could make out perches, and shapes on them.

"I've got three now," Zerbe said. "A peregrine, a gos, and a golden eagle."

The birds heard him, and shifted restlessly. One, the eagle I think, flew off its perch, came to the end of its leash, touched ground, and wheeled onto the perch again. Hanging on the wall, neatly, above the same oil cans and screwdrivers and rusty tire chain any of us might have in his garage, was the legendary equipment—the little hoods with bells, the lure bag, and the gauntlets.

Later, when we went out to fly the goshawk, I learned that the cage was for pigeons. Zerbe killed one before we left, stripping off the breast feathers to prepare it as a lure, exposing the flesh. He had weighed the goshawk; this was critical. If the bird were too full it might fly off and not come back. But it was down the required several ounces, therefore hungry enough to be lured, and we went out to a vast, meadowy hillside, taking two live pigeons in a gunnysack.

"If we were hunting freely now," Zerbe said, "and I weren't too concerned with losing the hawk, we'd send her up and cast off dogs at the same time. We'd follow the dogs, just as you would with your gun. When the dogs flushed a pheasant or a rabbit, the hawk would stoop, knock it down, and kill it; then I'd call her to me with the lure, you see, and the dogs would hold till I had her back, and then retrieve."

After that, he gave me the two live pigeons to hold, and released the goshawk.

"Keep those pigeons hidden in your shirt," he warned me, and though I didn't really understand the warning, I complied. The hawk circled upwards, slowly at first, then faster in tighter circles, and went completely out of sight, up in the light clouds somewhere. I was puzzled, and wondered if I should now commiserate on a lost bird, when Zerbe signaled me to toss a pigeon up. I did. The pigeon snapped its wings a few times, made a level circle all the way around us, and then started off, low and intent, to the west. With this the goshawk came bolting out of invisibility, so fast that the increase in her apparent size was continuous and explosive, and plummeted past the pigeon, striking it obliquely, not solidly enough to knock it down. The pigeon veered and stroked off, the hawk, recovering unbelievably, right after it, but in a contest at level flight the pigeon's ability to make shorter turns was decisive and it got away. The hawk settled onto a tree.

I looked at Zerbe, who was smiling ecstatically, quite undismayed, and who now began to whistle and to swing the dead pigeon lure around and thump it on the ground. Apparently it didn't matter much to him whether a kill was made or not, so I relaxed and smiled, too.

[8]

"Look out," he shouted just then. The big hawk had started towards us. "Your shirt. Your shirt." I remembered, just in time, and stuffed the second pigeon, which had gotten its head and shoulders out the gap between two buttons, back in place. Barely a second later the goshawk veered past me, enormous, its talons flared and terrifying, to land on Zerbe's lure and be recaptured. Later, it killed the second pigeon, and Zerbe told me there was a fair chance that, if I hadn't got it out of sight, I could have been badly injured. I saw the way the goshawk shot her talons completely through the lure pigeon's body, and agreed.

But I think of the garage when I think of modern falconing; the golden eagle perched near the child's discarded tricycle, the peregrine falcon silhouetted against the dusty window, and the smell of bird droppings and cold grease. And I know that this, whatever its pleasures, would not establish me as the Duke of York's descendant hunter. For Edward, there existed a perfect historical moment when need, ceremony, and pleasure came together. Even though I could build (or Zerbe could), if one of us were wealthy, a castle with a mew to keep the birds in, train a serf to be head falconer, import gyrfalcons from the Arctic and harpy eagles from the jungles, and follow them with red hounds on a piebald stallion—what an exposure of fantasy in the evening when the serf drove home to watch television, and in the morning mail with the Department of Agriculture wanting another health certificate for my eagle. There are fantasies in hunting, but my choice among them, as I shall acknowledge, lies elsewhere.

In our own, imperfect historical moment we inherit much conflict of attitude: there is what is still left of the Duke's joyfully ritual approach, as it declined into what the British call sportsmanship—a system of behavior which prescribes agreeable formalities towards other sportsmen, dictates which skills should be tested in a given hunting situation, proceeds by total restriction of the non-elite, and takes a point of view towards game which may, at times, be generous, and will, at others, permit the slaughter of hundreds of birds a day by an individual as long as it is done correctly. We inherit, with

[9]

equal strength, the meat-hunting attitude of the pioneer, part of it a response to the need for food, part of it sheer rebellion against the exclusive tradition of class-line sportsmanship; we inherit the free-shooting, fence-busting, wasteful spirit of the plainsman, and the greed of the buffalo and other market-hunters. All these involve, if not a contempt for game, at least a stupid indifference towards it, for they are attitudes towards man, not nature.

On the better side, as if these conflicting inheritances weren't enough, we derive a nice, if boyish, love of woodsman-ship from our romanticization of the Indian life which ours demolished. But best of all, we have conceived, as a significant national view, a genuine, if often frustrated, love for nature and for wildlife, and it is this which, at our best, we take hunting with us.

It is certainly incorrect to pick out a single source as the origin of what is most admirable in our confused hunting attitudes. But I find myself convinced that we are evolving an alternative to sportsmanship, which involves trying to fit into nature rather than reduce it to a game of skill (though it can't help but carry certain elements of the latter). And if this is so, then I think the possibility was opened for us at yet another historical moment, the one which sometimes comes just before it's too late, in the work and life of Henry Thoreau.

But what, before we come to Thoreau, has all this discussion of an ancient duke to do with the intention of this book of mine (for it is the chief function of this chapter to describe intentions)? Nothing at all, of course, except to provide a whole series of those useful negatives which define. For there is a tradition in sporting books, as I mentioned in my note, and here is the place where I can show how completely I fail to fit it. To paraphrase from Roderick Haig-Brown (in a splendid fishing book, called *A River Never Sleeps*), and mostly in his words, the great pattern for sporting books, set by the Duke of York's *The Master of Game*—you will recognize it if you re-member Isaac Walton—goes like this: The particular sport is compared to other, similar sports, much to its own advantage. Its delights are described, along with the virtues it breeds in men. It moves from there to technical information, turning

[10]

again to restate and emphasize the first point "in the light of the reader's grown knowledge of the subject."

Working backwards through that description, I find no comfortable point at which my own book will touch pattern. The reader will not know much more about hunting when I am done, only an odd thing or two that I've observed. The technical information will be nontechnical, and not very informative. Far from asserting that my sport is a breeder of virtues in men, I shall find myself implying that a grown-up American with a sporting gun in his hand is often declining towards moral idiocy. What I shall describe as hunting's delights may well be as incomprehensible to you (if you are not a hunter— *or even if you are*) as the description of one's infatuation with an ugly and worthless woman. Nor can I compare hunting to other sports to its advantage, for I think that skiing is cleaner, bird study gentler, most games better exercise, trout fishing more continuously absorbing . . . but my infatuation is what it is, and though you might persuade me of the ugliness and worthlessness of its object, was any lover ever persuaded to be out of love?

It seems a little mechanical, I admit, but since I am dealing here with five writers, and offering afterwards five more chapters, perhaps I may distribute dedications, picking for each writer that chapter which seems to me to correspond in some way with what I have learned from thinking about him. There are a few such points of correspondence for the Duke of York, perhaps, in my fourth chapter, which touches briefly on ceremonies of hunting and their lack; since it's five hundred years too late for him to feel that such familiarity is impertinent, I dedicate the chapter to him.

". . . despair is concealed even under what are called the games and amusements of mankind," Thoreau wrote, and (I am mixing two other passages from *Walden*): "Our lives are domestic in more senses than we think. From hearth to field is a great distance. . . . The very simplicity and nakedness of man's life in the primitive ages imply this advantage at least, that they left him still but a sojourner in nature."

I cannot avoid thinking that these lines, written about

[11]

nineteenth-century American life, come truer all the time. The pervasive despair, to begin with, seems very close to the surface now, hardly even concealed, in the compulsive way we pursue all our games and amusements, certainly including the instinct sports, which are hunting, fishing, and gathering. (Gathering: searching out mushrooms, nuts, berries—basically it is one of the set of instinctual imperatives which say to the armed child, or childish man: "If it moves, kill it; if it swims, catch it; if it grows, pick it; if it's lying on the ground, take it home.") It seems to me probable that it is because they give play to these instincts in an acceptable form that those of us who follow them so love the field sports. But there is pressure in two directions away from acceptable behavior. One urges us to revert to the primitive imperatives, which pushes towards anxiety—trouble with game wardens, the contempt of decent hunters. The other—and because most men act decently, either from fear of trouble or because they were raised that way, it is more common—is to pervert the instinct sports into something competitive. To describe the sort of desperation this leads to, Thoreau might have found use for the contemporary word "neurosis."

The competitiveness, in one of its forms, comes directly from the closing in of the American landscape, so that one may seldom hunt or fish (or even gather, for that matter) out of sight of others. Want to score? Be there first. Act quickly; if it makes for waste, so what? Someone there before you? Move in on him; he doesn't own the covert, the position on the stream; he might be getting something you could get. Outspend him; hire a better guide; shoot on a preserve; buy a faster boat; fire first with the biggest gun, the longest-range shells; fly in farther. Beat the bastard out, however you have to do it. (It is well that we democratize, but where are we to learn grace? Or doesn't it matter?) Generally I am aware enough of these impulses so that I can avoid the circumstances that stimulate them, the worst of it being that, like any neurotic pattern, it spoils the pleasure it's supposed to obtain. I avoid it not by strength of character but by being very wary of hunting or fishing on weekends, and by being willing to walk a mile or two away from roads. But sometimes my wariness lapses—once, last year, I had located a bed of strawberries gone wild, near an abandoned farm. I thought the knowledge must be mine exclusively, and drove out next day, with enthusiastic children, and cups to pick into, greedy as anyone. And as I drove up, saw a car parked nearby, assumed —wrongly, it turned out—that someone was after my berries. Imagine a forty-year-old man, of relatively even temperament, so perturbed at such a turn of expectations that he swings his own car wildly into a ditch, punishing himself and all those with him?

The other form of competitiveness that seems to me to lead to neurosis and despair is the curious American abhorrence of doing things alone. Every man must have his buddy, and the relationship, in a well-established case of buddihood, is very nearly as complicated as a marriage. The line at which a working companionship stops, and buddihood begins, could perhaps be drawn between two points: is there a particular companion, or companions, without whom it wouldn't be fun to go out? Being out, is the play and counterplay within the relationship allowed to become more absorbing than the hunting? Perhaps it isn't all wrong, in the sense of spoiling pleasure, if these things are so—I remember one season when I was more than halfway along towards buddihood, and there were some very agreeable things about it. But finally the inevitable comparison of performances made it too much like playing a daily game, keeping score, being one up or one down—thus, another of the hunting attitudes which is more concerned with man than with nature; the primitive hunter worked by himself, and for himself, and I cannot imagine him being despondent, so long as he got his mastodon, that Ugg's weighed more or Wugg's had longer tusks.

If competitiveness is one of the perversions leading to neurotic behavior in the instinct sports, another is that the distance Thoreau noted between hearth and field has changed in a curious way; it is as if we had tried to negate the distance by ignoring one of the poles. We no longer leave the hearth for the field; we take the hearth with us, wherever we go. The cars in which we drive out to hunt or fish are extensions of the hearth, and few men ever hunt out of sight of them. There

[13]

are hearth-gadgets, even, which come out of the car—stools to sit on, transistor radios in the duck blind on Saturday afternoon, so as not to miss the football game (television next?). There is conversation, which some companions cannot seem to help offering, about related things (dogs I once had, shots I made, things I saw, alibis I now offer), or even unrelated things. There is (and a tremendous amount of this) driving around—looking for particular spots, asking strangers for information, stopping for beer or cigarettes or candy bars, looking for game out the car window—so many things of the hearth which deny there is a field, and so decline the offer hunting makes: at best, hunting, like sleep, lets you leave your social self behind.

And finally, what is the field when we do get there, covering the vast psychological distance somehow, but another sort of hearth extension, the Great American Dump? "Domestic in more senses than we think," we are obdurately, querulously, spitefully, covering our continent with a thin geological layer of rusty metal, broken glass, and silt (having, in a former era, divided it with carelessly cruel barbed wire fences and posted it with didactic signs); thus we are insisting, essentially, that what of nature is not divided into rooms, with instructions for their use, must take on the domestic function of a repository for all the cess and waste of our bad lives. How long will the wildflowers continue to push their way up through the cracks? How long can the ducks continue to bring their flash of wild beauty to the trash river I hunt along, the Iowa, where flows the poison of a dozen cities, a hundred towns and ten thousand farms? Army engineers have built a huge dam here, the delight of water skiers, and the builders play with the water level in the name of flood control, raising it to drown the pheasant nests, lowering it to strand the duck nests, throwing in thousands of fish one week for public-relations purposes, and killing them the next through excessive fluctuation, destroying timber and grass and finally—so goes one theory which I like in a morose way without knowing whether it's true or not—silting in the basin of the lake they've made at such a rate that the lake itself cannot last more than a couple of dozen years. Admittedly, they have opened a lot of land in doing this—the government approach to nature is to give and take away about equally—and as for the silt, it came first, long before the engineers; it's been generations, such have soil and forest practices been out here, since anybody saw the bottom of the Iowa river through all the mud it carries. It's hard to imagine that anyone will ever see the bottom again, though it may not matter too much: to judge from the way this bottom feels, under the soles of a pair of hip boots, with its century's accumulation of abandoned farm machinery and pieces of old docks and the containers from a hundred years of picnics (does it give you a real sense of the American heritage to go where Grandpa broke his doxie's Moxie to sling your sweetie's Schlitz?)—I don't suppose the riverbed, through clear water, would be a pleasant sight.

This is the setting, these the conditions, which make for desperation or, to insist on my stodgy twentieth-centurism, neurotic behavior when we hunt, fish, or walk in the woods. I will name a few particular, specimen neuroses later (The Doctor Syndrome, The St. Valentine's Day Psychosis, The Rhinoceros Horn Complex)—and I will name my own. But I have not yet named the alternative I spoke about to the British ideal of the sportsman, and as a matter of fact I do not need to. Thoreau has done that for me: "A sojourner in nature," he calls him, one who stays in nature for a time, trying to fit rather than mar it, learning from it, taking from it, perhaps, a token or two—something good to eat, or hard to catch—as evidence for himself that he has understood something of how nature works and how a primitive self might use it.

There is, in this, not sport so much as self-renewal, an acknowledgement that one is of natural origin and belongs first to a world built by forces, not by hands; and the hunting, which gives shape and purpose to the sojourn, becomes a rite of simplification, in relief of our over-connected domestic and working lives.

Thoreau himself, of course, was the great sojourner, and the detail which will interest hunters is that, contrary to the impression one gets from Emerson, he was not a doctrinaire vegetarian. In *A Week on the Concord and Merrimac Rivers* he describes how he and his brother depended a good deal on

[15]

hunting for their food. During the first of the Walden years his avoidance of meat was part of his own program of simplification, and had nothing to do with sentimentalizing over other creatures; by the second year there, he was catching fish to supplement the vegetable diet, buying pork and lard occasionally, and he even reports killing and eating a groundhog at one point. Chiefly, his feeling towards wildlife was a great scholar's love for and curiosity about his subject (an attitude which is useless if there is anything sentimental in it); and he was marvelously endowed to act on this feeling, a consummate woodsman of whom a friend once remarked: "It was as if a man had once more come into Nature who knew what Nature meant him to do with her."

I would, as must be clear enough, far rather be like Thoreau when I go hunting than like the Duke of York (or like Turgenev, or Hemingway, with whom I shall begin to deal—

DANGEROUS QUARRY
[16]

somewhat more briefly—in a moment). Yet identification would again be wishful and remote; the kindest a friend might say about my outdoor performance would be something like: "He doesn't get water in his boots *every* time he wades a stream; after he has exhaustively identified an unknown mushroom from his several field guides and determined that it's edible, it's true he generally discards it anyway—but once he didn't; and he made really a very good shot at long range on a pheasant two seasons ago (or perhaps it was three)." It's as if a man had once more come into nature whom nature knew how to bully—but when I look around me, I see that I am not alone.

Since I cannot handle nature like Thoreau, I am not fit to observe nature like Thoreau, and my book—unlike his works—will not be full of those superbly casual first-hand revelations of the ways in which birds and animals live and move. Perhaps, though, as a novelist, I have some training in observing the lives and movements of men; insofar as this volume has anything in it of the natural history at which Thoreau was so very good, it may contain some rough notes towards a natural history of hunters. With this in mind, it seems I might dedicate any of the chapters to Thoreau, but particularly the first, since it has the widest variety of situations and specimens in it, and covers various metamorphic stages of the chief specimen, which is myself.

It is of some comfort, in choosing lives with which to compare one's own, to pick two at once: an unattainable ideal, and one which can in some respects be matched. If, at my best as a hunter, I am nothing like Thoreau, then perhaps I am something like Ivan Turgenev.

The Russian novelist was born within fifteen months of the American naturalist, though I doubt that either ever heard of the other, and their social environments were completely different. Nineteenth-century Russia was a country of a few landowners and many serfs, and I would suppose that Turgenev, who belonged to the landowning class, began his hunting in emulation of the Western European high style that influenced his personal life in many ways—as a young American today might take up shooting birds because it has some-

[17]

thing fashionable about it. (Ah, the moment when one first steps into the Abercrombie and Fitch gun room thinking: "Yes, yes. It's for me. I'm a charge customer here, me; yes.!")

If Turgenev did begin with some such nonsense, there is none of it left in his famous collection of pieces with hunting backgrounds, called *A Sportsman's Notebook*. It's a book which has often been picked by other writers as his finest. Sherwood Anderson called it "the sweetest thing in all literature," and may have had it in mind to some extent when he wrote the *Winesburg, Ohio* stories. Hemingway was referring to it, I'm fairly certain, when he spoke of having beat old man Turgenev in a fair fight—I assume the comparison was between *A Sportsman's Notebook* and the Michigan stories, but they're not really comparable. Hemingway's are nostalgic stories, Turgenev's nostalgic memoirs—it's a little like claiming to have beat another man arm-wrestling when all the other man meant to do was shake hands.

The image one gets of Turgenev's hunting, from his sketches, is one of straightforward enjoyment and perfect, simple adjustment; he is hunting because he likes to, likes the exercise and the countryside, and it never occurs to him that any of this need be questioned. It is the background, even and agreeable, for the meetings he has with serfs—odd people, many of them, but thoroughly human—and part of the fame of *A Sportsman's Notebook* is that it played, in a much quieter way, an *Uncle Tom's Cabin*-like role in the political movement which brought freedom to the serfs of Russia; no one had ever described them as humans before. But the very placidity with which *A Sportsman's Notebook* deals with hunting makes it no model for another hunting book; hunting is something pleasant and absorbing, but quite personal, that is going on, a pursuit in which the reader is not expected to feel a high degree of interest. From time to time, in its pages, a bird flies up—a snipe or blackcock; Turgenev drops it, and goes on with the discussion of the fascinating or pathetic peasant characters he feels will interest us more.

From a reader's standpoint, the book is a marvel; from a hunter's, it is rather disappointing except for a single chapter in which Turgenev has to settle for shooting ducks, which seems to him unsporting, and has mishaps enough so that the hours on the pond seem to him worth describing in detail.

Now and then when I go hunting, it seems to me I am taking it all as easily and openly as Turgenev, and I have tried to get at this a little in the chapter called "The Fields Near Home," which I dedicate to him.

Only one of the Hemingway stories which the author seems to have used in comparing himself to Turgenev deals directly with hunting or fishing. It is the story called "Big, Two-Hearted River" and though this turns on a very small point, it's a sharp enough one to begin to prick at the over-inflated critical view that Hemingway's heroes are to be understood in terms of their adherence to and departures from strict codes of behavior: for in the story Nick Adams, a hero very closely identified with Hemingway, is fishing for trout, pretty efficiently but rather impurely. He ignores the flybook he has with him and uses live grasshoppers for bait, giving no consideration at all to the sporting code which the critics' Hemingway would surely have used as a touchstone. I was a little surprised at Nick, as a matter of fact, on rereading the story, which shows the foolishness of letting ourselves be taught assumptions; it is sometimes a good idea to look at what a man actually wrote, rather than relying on what people say he wrote.

In Hemingway, one may look at the fishing passage (trout again) in *The Sun Also Rises,* the fine account of duckshooting in *Across the River and into the Trees.* Then there's the deep-sea-fishing scene in *To Have and Have Not* to which, now that I think about it, I will have to acknowledge some indebtedness, for it must have been the first thing I ever read in which a self-styled sportsman is acting disagreeably—well, yes, neunotically—hell, I wish I hadn't remembered it; I didn't as a matter of fact, until the very last revision of this chapter. *The Old Man and the Sea* is, of course, a fishing story, though the old man's purpose out there is commerce rather than sport, and the writer's purpose probably something more than telling the tale of a hard day at the oars. Finally there is one Hemingway book which deals exclusively with sporting matters, and surely that is where to look to learn how he hunted and how he felt about it; that is the big-game book, *Green Hills of Africa*.

Let me describe the book first, for though it is often dismissed as a poor piece of work I do not find it so. I like it, myself; it's a book which, in my judgement, achieves very well the purpose set forth—to try "to write an absolutely true book to see whether the shape of a country and the pattern of a month's actions can, if truly presented, compete with a work of the imagination." To me it competes reasonably well; unlike those who reached first and second judgements of it, we are far enough away from Hemingway to take his role in the book as it should be taken—as that of a chief character, rather than that of an actual man self-exposed to our endearing hunger for the material of gossip.

Now that Hemingway has passed from envied rival to revered ancestor (and most of his rivals with him), I suggest that the most interesting thing in *Green Hills* is not what the I-character says in a spiteful moment about Gertrude Stein (who may some day require a footnote to identify her in scholarly editions of Hemingway's works). The most interesting thing is precisely what the book has in common with good novels—vivid, complicated, and appealing people, involved in something they care deeply about. Certainly the I-character is momentarily spiteful—he is also boastful, a self-admitted show off, and afraid of snakes—and along with this a sensitive, skillful man who loves nearly every moment of what he is doing in the book, and loves the people with whom he does it. These are principally his wife (and it adds nothing at all to know outside of context that it was his second wife, that she was a Catholic, and so on—for these characteristics have nothing to do with the woman in the book); the droll and dignified white hunter whom the I-character calls Pop; and the native tracker M'Cola. Does it matter that the man on whom the I-character is based is going to win the Nobel prize one day, and, on another, commit suicide? No; those are other stories, as irrelevant to judging *Green Hills* as being able to remember the name of the woman on whom Lady Brett is based is irrelevant to judging *The Sun Also Rises*. What matters about the I-character in *Green Hills* is only what is in the book: His marvelous enthusiasm for Africa, his being victim of several rather funny running jokes with which Pop and his wife deflate him as the month goes on, his capacity to become depressed by a friend's bad luck, his resilience, his tenacity as a hunter.

The direct material for literary gossip, which probably accounts for ninety per cent of the comment on *Green Hills*, occupies about three per cent of the text, ten pages out of 295. The rest is hunting, thinking, shooting, excitement, observation of Africa, and affectionate exchange, and it all becomes so very vivid that I have wondered if it ought not to have been published simply as a novel. For certainly the pleasure in reading it is in taking it as a particular kind of fiction, not as a look into the laundry basket of a prominent man.

If it is taken my way, then it is quite simple to know how to read those paragraphs which comprise the three per cent— the paragraphs of facile comment about "writing without tricks and without cheating," those often plagiarized pages in which American literature is summed up, and the few remarks about people like Miss Stein. In the context of the book, they are part of a carefully prepared, rather comic scene: I-character is drinking strong beer, tired from a day's hunting. He is being pushed by an ill-met stranger, who is nice, serious and a bore—one who dislikes hunting and never drinks— pushed into talking more, and with a greater attempt at seriousness, than the hunter is really up to. The quality in this dialogue which seems to me more striking, really, than those parts of its content which are lifted out for solemn or jeering repetition, is the extraordinary courtesy with which the I-character responds to the bore, a courtesy which both his wife and Pop clearly feel unnecessary. They are trying to protect the sensitive boaster from that self-revelation unto nakedness into which, when we are unwary from drink and tiredness, a stranger's serious attentiveness can push any of us.

Read that way, the scene is a beautifully done, minor piece of a remarkably live book about a hunting party after kudu, sable, buffalo—a book full of hard tracking, good and bad shots, diversions, frustrations, jokes, and deep pleasures in a haunting landscape. I think the critics would do well to look at *Green Hills of Africa* again. I think it may come to be ranked fairly high among Hemingway's works—not on the same level with *The Sun Also Rises, A Farewell to Arms,* and the best dozen of the stories, but just below them. Hemingway produced a solid, second-level book in *Green Hills,* and our literature would be one good volume poorer without it.

But for all my admiration (and I would not be able to make such a guess were not the I-character of *Green Hills* made so clear), I cannot tell myself that Hemingway would have had much use for me as a hunting companion. He was no sojourner—in many ways, the safari with its elaborate equipment, transportable comforts, and complete reliance on professional experts and native labor, seems to me the opposite of the sojourn. As *Walden* was the ultimate in sojourning, so a safari seems the ultimate in sportsmanship, and Hemingway seems to have liked it all immensely: the competitiveness, the occasional not-quite-necessary tests of courage and endurance, the trophy collecting. He was, I am sure, a good deal better shot and perhaps a more patient hunter than I (I grow restless when I try to still-hunt); and—this may be part of being better at it—he was capable of certain things which seem crude to me, even brutal. The sojourner and the sportsman can hunt happily together only if the latter is uncompetitive and if the former will adhere (there is no contradiction involved) to the sportsman's code and I am, in intention, half one and half the other. But Hemingway, and I know of no way to account for this except in terms of the boyish American preference for efficiency over tenderness, was no more an adherent than was Nick Adams in his fishing. My reference is *Green Hills of Africa,* page 133: the I-character and M'Cola are standing in an African lake, shooting ducks, "... then they come whistling back, passing faster than you can load and shoot, and you brown a bunch to get cripples for decoys and then take only fancy shots ..."

There it is, and I shan't try to say any more about it, except that I hope my describing it will be taken as an unprejudiced effort to understand, like an interest in Dostoyevsky's gambling or Proust's snobbery. I can only add, after reporting that he killed the four crippled ducks shortly afterwards, that it is a kind of evasion of the sportman's code that I have seen many times, in many forms, and in myself as well (. . . but the water is high and muddy, and nothing is rising, and you look around to make sure nobody's watching and take the Ginger Quill off your leader and tie on a hook, and you turn a stone and the worm is there. . . .) It is the final thing which makes me doubt that sportsmanship is an idea adaptable to American culture, and convinces me that we had better teach our children to be sojourners if we can.

Well. I have not tried to write a book like *Green Hills*. My hunting experiences are insufficiently consecutive, and I have had to use a form I worked out for myself in another book, in which the lines between story, essay, and autobiography are not acknowledged. But it would be silly for me to try to deny that Hemingway's influence is in the form somewhere, and very likely the language too, as it was silly of me to have forgotten, for a time, the scene I mentioned in *To Have and Have Not*.

I never met Hemingway or even saw him. He was reported to hold a good opinion of my writing, for which I am grateful. If there is a chapter here fit to dedicate to him, it would be the last, for there are some tests and dangers indicated there (albeit inadvertent ones), and the chapter is about death. Death, not codes, was Hemingway's subject; it was a country he knew how to hunt, and from which he brought back the great trophies which are his major books.

Now we come to Nathanael West, one writer, after all, who hunted birds, with whom I do identify although—more likely because—he never, so far as I know, wrote about it. If you are reading this book because you are a hunter, and reading these paragraphs out of some sort of kindly curiosity, it is likely you have not heard much about West. Like so much that is good and bad in our culture, reputations are manufactured here more often than won, and the namewrights have not yet fixed him up a fame to match his stature. Since you are a twentieth-century human being, literary or not, I could recommend two of West's novels to you, *Miss Lonelyhearts* and *The Day of the Locust,* as among the best of our times— sardonic, visionary romances of the thirties, hard-bitten, masterfully imagined and controlled, hitting the most elusive of the winged targets writers point at: love, hope, illusion, evil. The wisecrack was the characteristic form of expression in those depressed days, and these books are like apocalyptic wisecracks in their bitter conception, their perfect delivery, and their ineluctable pertinence.

I know of West's bird-hunting from two sources, both half-forgotten now, and have obviously imagined him a hunter in my image out of the very forgetfulness, and the deep feeling I have for his work. One source was a long story, by Josephine Herbst, based on West and called "The Hunter in the Sky." (I wish it had not been ten years since I read it; I wish I had it to read again.)

In the story Miss Herbst's character (as I remember it, or have re-imagined it) went out day after day, alone, with dog and gun. Would be seen, perhaps, crossing a fence, holding the wires apart for his dog. Would be gone for hours, and no one knew when he came back from wherever it was (but now and then would see an evening silhouette, moving along a ridge line, against the sky, and supposed it must be West, quietly returning.) This took place, one understood, in a community of people who knew one another well, and where none of the rest hunted, or could imagine, or cared very much, why West did. It was a romantic image I took from the story, like a calendar illustration called "The Hunter and his Dog at Dusk," though what I took may have been quite different from what Miss Herbst put in—this often happens with good writing.

A few years later I read an article by Malcom Cowley about Nathanael West and his works, which was part reminiscence, part review, and learned from it that West had not been a particularly effective hunter in the sense of bringing home a lot of meat, and that the dog he took along turned out to be no bird dog, really, just a hound that tagged along. It may be unfair to West's memory—he may have been a better shot than Hemingway, a better-adjusted hunter than Turgenev, a more knowledgeable woodsman than Thoreau, and more ceremonious than the old Duke—but reading the Cowley piece gave me the most comforting of all the images of other men I carry around with me to feed my own neurosis: it is the image of a man like myself, a sojourner in fantasy. For if I sometimes feel that I understand something of the habits of game, or behave correctly in a satisfying way, still, most of my hours as a hunter are spent in revery improvised to fit the circumstance. I am acting roles, many various ones, and the great advantages are that I am my only audience, perfectly satisfied with the performance, and that the scenery is real. I am alone, often, and need to be, walking the great distance Thoreau noted between hearth and field, transported out of myself into all the strange selves I need to learn about for my own reassurance. If a bird fall, it is like being able to bring back a token from a dream.

Since I feel so much of fool's certainty that Nathanael West must have found this in hunting, too, and must therefore have encountered situations from time to time wherein he met, dismayingly, men with opposed fantasies or real purposes, I should like to dedicate "The Goose Pits" to him, for it goes into these things further.

If the pleasure of going hunting often is for me, as I've admitted, that of acting a series of roles in a continuous private play with real scenery, then I would also have to admit that it's a fairly neurotic kind of pleasure. Like any of the ones based on unreality, it becomes pleasure's opposite when the film breaks—that is, when something happens to challenge its fragile connection to fact. Any sort of mishandling of a hunting situation which I commit can expose that despair which Thoreau points out, for that, it seems, is what the fantasy covers.

Yet I do not see that hunting is less neurotic for other Americans, only that their neuroses take different forms, using a wide definition of "neurosis" as meaning any consistent, inappropriate pattern of response to a certain kind of opportunity.

I shan't examine all the forms I've seen; in fact, I shall take only three (besides my own) as representative, and the first of these I should call hunting for status, or The Doctor Syndrome.

There is a group of doctors, to illustrate, in a small, midwestern city, who have bought up a duck marsh forty miles away and built a clubhouse (a lot of marshes and clubhouses are being bought up by doctors these days). The son of one of them, a boy I know quite well, went down with his father and the others one weekend and told me the rest of this:

"My God," he said. "I've never had such duck shooting. There were five men there, and a pusher they hire to stay in the clubhouse and call and cook for them, and the limit was four ducks. That made twenty-eight ducks we were allowed per day, and fifty-six in possession. Well, the pusher could shoot his during the week if he wanted, when no one was around, and they more or less let him understand that he was to give up his limit to the rest over the weekend—not that he seemed to care much.

"We got in Friday evening, and there were ducks all over the sky—the migration was coming through, the weather was just right, there couldn't have been another week end like it that year. Friday night, Dad and the others started drinking and playing cards, but I'd been studying all fall instead of hunting. I really wanted to shoot ducks. So I went to bed.

"Saturday I got up at 4:30, and the only other man who'd even go out to the blind with me was the old pusher. Most of those men were just plain passed out, more or less where they'd been drinking, though I was relieved to see Dad had crawled into a bunk and got most of his clothes off. You know, it's really pretty to watch him shoot, and he used to really like it, but he wouldn't get up.

"So the pusher and I went out to the blind, and stayed all morning, him calling and me shooting, and none of them ever showed up. I took eighteen ducks, all by myself. Saturday evening I went out again; two went with me, but one was half-lit and fooling around and the other was Dad—he'd had a few drinks and wouldn't do anything but watch. It made me nervous, and I missed a lot and only took three; the guy that

[26]

was fooling around might have doubled with me on one.

"Saturday night they got drunk again, and Sunday morning Dad had promised he'd go out but he said when I woke him that he felt too sick. One of the others came out the door of the clubhouse, and said it was too damn wet and cold, he'd come later on, and went back to bed. Of course he never came. You'd think I'd have liked it, having all that shooting to myself, but I don't know—anyway, I shot forty-one that weekend, and maybe doubled on the forty-second, you've never seen such hunting. Then we split them up among all the doctors when we got ready to leave, and on the way home Dad and I stopped for coffee at the place near town where they all know him. And somebody said, very enviously:

" 'Good hunting this weekend, Doc?'

"And Dad said: 'Everybody's got birds to take home,' and I felt funny as hell about it, all those men sitting there smiling kind of ass-kissing smiles, wishing they could get asked to go along some time and shoot beside the doctors."

The St. Valentine's Day Psychosis is a little more serious, though my first example of it is rather funny. It concerns a genuine Chicago gangster I read about last fall in the newspapers. He and a couple of assistant thugs had been dove hunting, down in Arkansas I think it was, and were stopped by the game warden. The limit on doves was twelve per day, twenty-four in possession, which is pretty generous, entitling the three men to seventy-two. And seventy-two were what they showed the warden which indicated a staggering number of shells must have been shot—real gangsters may be better with guns than the average hunter, but still, the average man knocks down about three doves per twenty-five shells. And what would you suppose the warden found when he made them open the trunk of the long, black, get-away Cadillac? Over five hundred more dead doves.

My other example is that of the boy who drove a garbage truck out in Nebraska—this was about five years ago. He was somewhat defective mentally, apparently, but was said to be a tremendous shot. He began demonstrating on people one day, and by the time three days were past had killed eleven. Started out with people he knew, and took the others about

[27]

as he and his girl could jump them—I can imagine what he must have been like as a hunting partner before that.

I think of the men who hunt all dressed up like Englishmen, or all dressed up like Texans, but the third neurosis I want to name is the one of which non-hunting women like to accuse their husbands, or other connections: The Rhinoceros-Horn Complex. The rhinoceros, as you may have read, is very nearly extinct, it has been hunted so hard by natives of its region, because the horn on its nose is believed to provide material, in dried and powered form, for aphrodisiacs. The mistake these naïve hunters make is not really much different, though a little less abstract, from the mistake made by the men who like to appear as hunters because it seems to them to advertise their own virility. And while I think women occasionally see examples of this where it doesn't really exist, I certainly wouldn't deny that it exists at all . . . the gun as penis, the shot as ejaculation, the sadism gratified in the kill . . . yes, it's there all right; there are even certain females who accept the image with some corresponding excitement.

I think, finally, of the men who turn their interest in hunting into schemes for making money—but this is perversion, really, rather than neurosis—gun-dealers, dog-breeders, men with business on their mind, guides, (sporting writers? all right) and all the rest. Surely nothing can spoil a pleasure more thoroughly than pursuing it for gain.

So, finally, I think of the old tag which comes up from time to time in conversation, or more often in the ads of weapons-manufacturers: "Allah does not count, in a man's allotted span, the hours spent in hunting." (Manufacturers of fishing equipment change the final word.) In the inevitable way of old tags, this one seems sometimes to be true: there are such hours, marvelous, absorbed, stolen from time.

But there are so many others: hysteric hours, compulsive hours, greedy hours, competitive hours, play-acting hours; hours of impatience and anger; hours of boredom and discomfort and frustration; hours in which success and failure take on disproportionate importance; dishonest and unhappy hours—hours which I feel sure an Allah would count double.

I shall try to describe some of both kinds, good hours and bad, in the chapters that follow.

[28]

2. Opening Days

ON OPENING DAY OF THE DOVE SEASON IN TEXAS,
so the newspapers report, gunners stand
shoulder to shoulder on certain country
roads, taking birds with a concentration of fire which often
disintegrates the targets in the air. On opening day of the
trout season on the Beaverkill, in New York, one may read
that fishermen push and jostle one another along the cold
and muddy banks like the crowd at a Southern baptism.

I hope never to see either of these events. The important
openings in my locality, which is east central Iowa, about
fifty miles west of the Mississippi River, are those of duck
and pheasant seasons; and while the crush of sportsmen and
the crash of guns is not so sensational as to bring out report-
ers, they are not good days. Too much tension is accumulated
in each of us through the yearning months when we must
leave the shotguns home—we mend boots, see birds fly out in
front of dogs in training, shoot clay sometimes, thumb cata-
logues wishing for thousand-dollar guns, and wear out one
another's reminiscences. Finally anticipation gorges us so,

as we wait, straining at watches towards the legal minute on an autumn Saturday, that its discharge has a kind of viciousness as incompatible with the enjoyment of a beloved sport as it is inappropriate to the harmlessness of the birds which are its victims.

"Got the son-of-a-bitch," we cry (or "missed") as if the bird had done us injury.

Of the half-dozen opening days of various sorts which I remember in particular—almost all are concerned with ducks—there is one which I recall with decidedly strained amusement, and only one whose recollection gives me real pleasure. Last year's duck opening out here may stand for all the rest.

i.

The opening I try to find amusing took place eleven years ago, in northern Florida, and was a personal re-opening for me. I had not hunted or fished since boyhood, and I wouldn't want to suggest that I was precociously skilled or devoted then. Any kid with a twenty-two rifle who spends his summer in the woods, does what my brothers and I did—pots a rabbit or a groundhog now and then, misses a good many others. He may dig some worms and try fishing if there's a creek nearby, and the day will come when he's allowed to come along on a quail hunt and learns to fear the kick of a twenty-gauge shotgun unduly, not understanding that the stock is much too long for him to shoulder properly. He will conduct, during such summers, a boy's fitful investigation of the power to inflict death which most creatures have towards some other species and which only man has towards all. Man can kill anything, if he sets his mind to it, and he has—man the omnicide. But the boy will learn that most private men (whatever most individual cats or hawks or chiefs of state might do) will not wish to exercise the power indiscriminately simply because circumstances allow that it be done without punishment. I don't recall what agonized rabbit or gasping fish I may have learned this from. Mostly I remember how much I felt at home wading up the creek, sitting very still under a squirrel tree, riding an old horse into the Virginia mountains—these things were part of an environment with which I casually identified for a few months each year, never pausing to analyze how I felt towards it.

It seems to me now that I must have loved it better than I knew. For after the years between (in which, instead of going into the woods seeking game, I went to parties seeking girls; and into college, war, marriage, and the city, seeking manhood) I came so wholeheartedly back, in my late twenties, to a life in which I am, by now, outdoors doing something or other part of every day. When the gun's not legal, I work my dogs, or go fishing, hunt mushrooms or take the children out to look for birds and wildflowers. If my skill at and knowledge of such things are never likely to become extraordinary, the burgeoning of devotion has created a habit very like addiction, even a need like that for sleep.

I began to discover this progression in myself on the Florida visit which I mentioned. I had ten days to spend there, and circumstances threw me often into the company of a college boy named Abel Cassoway with whom, though he was a dozen years my junior, I became quite friendly. He asked one afternoon if I would like to go bass fishing. I said that I knew nothing about it, but that it sounded pleasant, and the next morning was up before sunrise for the first time since I'd left the Army. I found it strange, unexpectedly chilly and quite exhilarating.

We'd meant to spend only the morning fishing, but the day seized and carried us off—I called in at noon from the fishing camp on Cross Creek where we were eating cold sandwiches (the fastest food they had) to say we'd be back around three; we didn't actually see home again until after dark.

Cross Creek runs like a canal from one shallow lake to another, slow water with even slower backwaters from which stick up the cypress knees where bass loaf. There is, as I remember it, marsh grass and swamp trees, all sorts of shady tangle, and somewhere back in there on a tree, sometime in the afternoon, I saw a bird. I had taken, by then, the first obscure step towards the open air—I had begun to watch birds, and like most beginners in that discipline saw rare

[31]

ones everywhere. The one on the tree must of course be an Anhinga, which Abel would call a water turkey.

"What's the bird?" I cried; I was paddling at the time while he cast something called an Hawaiian wiggler, a frog-colored lure with a propeller on its front and a skirt of rubber strands. Actually, he was just then beginning to retrieve the lure, skittering it across the surface past a particularly large cypress knee.

He looked back at me, said "Where?", missed a strike and said "Damn." He brought the lure in, cast it to the same place, and it seemed as if the bass came out of the water to get it and save me an apology. It was a large, determined fish—a five-pound one it turned out—and it thrashed, darted, tugged, and leapt for several tense minutes before Abel could reel it over to the boat. When he finally had it in he said: "There, sorry. A bird?"

And I said: "Doesn't matter. I don't see him any more."

From then on Abel conscientiously pointed out and identified every bird he saw, including swallows and blackbirds, and at one point (now he was paddling while I tried to cast) said excitedly, "Four ducks!"

This time I cried "Where?", and if it didn't cause me to miss a strike, neither did it prevent me from catching a snag. I didn't see the ducks and Abel, interpreting my anxiety over the snag as frustration at missing the sight, and finding in this a reasonable extension of my curious interest in swallows and blackbirds, pronounced me a duck hunter.

"The season opens Friday," he said, and then in a comic backwoods voice he often affected: "Why right here's one best good place to shoot from, right up here in the lake, at the end of the creek. 'Course there ain't likely to be uhna ducks down yet, but I could get you the borrow of a gun."

Florida often opened up too early, he explained. It would take a real lot of cold weather up North to bring in migrant birds this soon. Local birds just wouldn't amount to much— I reminded him that I was leaving Saturday. If I was to go at all with him, and by now I was surprisingly agitated by the idea, Friday would have to be the day.

On Thursday afternoon Abel came with a college friend,

a big strong-armed man he called Perk, who looked as though he might be able to reach up and catch ducks with his bare hands. Abel had rounded up three shotguns, but one, a single shot with the stock taped together, didn't look too good to him, and he thought we'd better leave it back.

"I got it from an old colored man I gave our bass to," he said.

It was decided we three could take turns with the two sound guns; I reported that I'd arranged to borrow an outboard motor from our landlords at the cabin my wife and I were staying in. The only other preparation we made was to throw some green grapefruit up into the air for one another to shoot at—the memory of that long-stocked twenty-gauge was still with me and I wanted to get rid of it. Actually, Perk declined with a smile to try this exercise at all. I managed to expose my disclaimer of experience as being altogether true by missing four shots. Abel, when I hurled the fruit up and away, as hard as I could, hit it with the first barrel so that it jumped in the air, like a light plane hitting a pocket, spun for a moment round and golden green in the sunlight, and then flew into fragments against the sky when he took it again with the other barrel. Perk said mockingly: "My, my. Wasn't that nice?" Then they tossed an easy one for me, lobbing it slowly, and I actually hit the thing myself, putting a couple of stray pellets from the outside of my pattern into it as Abel proved when he picked it up and showed me the holes. I was secretly proud, though I calculated Perk was unimpressed— I took him for one of those people whose physical size and competence have the same effect as condescension but without giving one the same room for comforting resentment that intentional condescension gives.

The next morning I was up at three-thirty. I had been waiting so impatiently in my sleep for the alarm to sound that I woke and turned it off, certain it had rung. Then I noticed the position of the hands and realized it was set for half an hour later, dressed, tried to eat and couldn't; couldn't find anything else to do either, and so I went outdoors in the cool, dark Florida morning and sat beside the road waiting, the outboard motor next to me, my head full of the same inaccurate visions of sounding guns and falling birds which had prevented sleep so long when I'd gone self-consciously early to bed the night before. (Still, sometimes, in duck season, those same naïve visions come to me when I am early in bed and half-awake—uninformed, unrevised by experience; I don't know why.)

I was asleep by the road, slumped into the motor, when Abel and Perk drove up, promptly at four-fifteen. The season was to open a few minutes after five.

"Got a lunch?" Abel asked, when they'd waked me.

I shook my head.

"Gets hungry out there. Oh, I got enough for three." At this hour, in my overwrought state, his country grammar seemed natural, not comic, and quite reassuring—the men who supervised my boyhood shooting in Virginia spoke that way.

"I've got better than lunch," Perk said, holding up a paper sack which was twisted tight around the form of the bottle inside it, and Abel told him to put that thing away before it commenced to claw and bite him. I could pretty well reconstruct, as we drove off and it continued, the wrangle they'd been having over the bottle—at some point, it seemed, Perk had agreed not to open it till later but was still using it as a taunt.

There were no cars on the road, no lights at the farms, nothing moving at all until we came near the fishing camp on Cross Creek from which we'd hired our bass boat earlier that week. Now it was a duck camp and to turn onto its lane was to find oneself in a traffic jam in the middle of the woods just before dawn. We inched along, held back by cars ahead which were waiting for other cars to park, until finally Abel stopped and jumped out, calling that I should follow and Perk take care of the parking. By the time I caught up, Abel was already at the water's edge, claiming the boat he'd reserved. It was a big cypress boat and had a strip of wood screwed all the way around inside it, spaced out from the gunwales. At points in the space palmetto boughs had been stuck to form a screen but not enough, Abel said, not nearly enough, and he began pulling hasty handfuls of marsh grass and throwing them into the boat. It was the first time I'd seen him move at any pace other than deliberate. I caught his impatience and together we raced around the shore, snatching up stalks of grass, trying to get to what remained before others, who were running around and snatching grass in the same way. It was a weird little interval, there in the pre-dawn, and the arrival of Perk, looming up big and composed-looking with his paper bottle in one hand and the five-horse outboard held lightly in the other, made me resent him even more, for making Abel look silly and frantic.

We tumbled into the boat, in on top of the pile of grass we'd made, and Perk, still on shore, passed the motor to Abel to hook onto the stern. Then Perk gave a great shove at the bow and leapt in, too, and we were away, drifting. There was the usual hour-long minute trying to start an outboard when time seems short; then Abel got it going, and we went off. There were three other boats just ahead. The motion calmed me; I sighed, settled myself, glanced at the sky and couldn't find it. I hadn't noticed fog on land, but the air above the creek was saturated with it.

There were boats behind as well as ahead of us now, but I can't say how I knew—I could scarcely see them in the fog or hear them above the sound of our own motor. Two went by, after a time, at considerable speed, rocking us first from one side and then from the other, much too close; racing each other, Abel shouted, cursing them, for some hot spot on the lake. Hope they wind up shooting each other for it. Meanwhile, what in hell were Perk and I doing with the grass? The answer to that was that we were doing the best we could, thrusting handfuls of it around the palmetto stems, but they were really not close enough together to hold well and we lost a lot.

I'm not sure how I knew, when we reached it, that we had left the creek and were on the lake—the fog was lighter, perhaps, but not in density so much as color, white fog instead of grey. Yet it must have been thinner, too, for we could see the three intermittent boat shadows we'd been following split, and go off into what seemed to be channels; and when we'd moved a little closer, I could see that the channels were actually paths through the lake weeds and lily pads.

Abel cut the motor and we drifted in sudden silence,

[35]

watching the disappearing boats; then we were alone in the fog though behind us we could hear other motors coming up along the creek.

"I'll have to take a guess," Abel said. "Some of these lanes go clear across the lake, some might stop in thirty, forty yards." He started the motor again, nosed the boat along the edge of the weeds until we came to a lane and turned up it. "We'll just go as far as we can," he called, above the sound of the outboard, "and throw out the anchor."

I'd guess we went along slowly for about five minutes before the channel closed in front of us, and we stopped.

"Made it," Abel said, and by my watch there were still eight minutes to go before duck season opened. All three of us seemed calm now, as if getting here on time had been the test, and not the shooting which might follow. Abel and Perk pulled the outboard motor off the transom and laid it on the floor, as was required by law.

They even resumed what I took to be a more or less continuous, low-key wrangling which must characterize their friendship. "Suppose you did have decoys, where could you put them with all these weeds around?" Perk said.

"Bunches, anywhere around the boat. Maybe I'd have you crouch down up to your neck in water, and hold a pair up over your head for me."

"You couldn't see them if I did," Perk said. "But I guess the ducks would have their fog lights on."

That ran out; we fell silent and watched the time. Abel'd insisted that Perk and I were to have first turns with the guns. I sat in the stern, Perk in the bow, with Abel watching in the center of the boat. There were three minutes to go.

"You take back and left," Abel whispered. "Perk take front and right."

"You already said that," Perk whispered back. There were two minutes. It was light enough now to see that the fog thinned above the water; twenty feet above, it was thin enough to see it drift, and here and there I could make out a tall tree way off along some high point of shore line.

There was a minute; it passed. My second hand crossed the mark. The season was open and for a long moment there was no sound. Then from no particular direction way across the lake, wan and without vibration, the noise of six or seven shots floated by us.

"Someone got up on ducks resting," Abel whispered. "Took them on the water, soon as time came."

It was probably true. No birds were moving. There were no other shots, and again we sat in silence, straining our eyes towards what sky showed.

And then a bird materialized, flapping low and slowly towards us head-on, big-winged and deliberate.

"Is that a duck?" I whispered idiotically.

"Shitpoke," Abel said and just then it turned its unmistakable heron's silhouette and I hung my silly head.

A few more minutes went by. I saw birds high up, flying in a group, and uncertainly raised my gun.

"Crows," Abel said kindly.

Blackbirds swept by, in and out of the fog. A gull. And then four shapes, driving at us out of the mist with susurrating wings, urgent and unmistakable and gone before you could catch your breath, and something atavistic in me knew immediately what that sound was, that shaped shadow, so that I found myself whispering along with Abel:

"Those are ducks."

They were past us and out of sight before either Perk or I could mount his gun, but just before they disappeared we saw two split off. A moment later the two were back in sight again, climbing a little, turning to soar past us, and I saw with craven relief that they would go by the bow from right to left, Perk's shot not mine.

Into range they came, their wings stroking like machines, and Perk's gun was on them, following them, but the sound I was braced for never came. The big man sat there stiff, his gun to his shoulder, his back rigid. I could see sweat on his neck.

"Shoot! Shoot!" Abel yelled, a moment too late, but still Perk didn't move; then the ducks were gone.

And with that I understood and ached for Perk—understood his bottle and his casualness and even knew, or thought I did, his version of the naïve dream of hunting which prevents

[37]

SHOOTING IN TURN

sleep for the neophyte. (His dream might have this very moment, just past, in it, and he shoots, casually but superbly, and Abel cries, "Good shot!" and Perk says, "You damn fool. I never had a shotgun in my hands before.") His gun came down, his big face turned apologetically, questioningly towards us, but three startling reports cut off whatever he was going to say. They seemed so close that I thought Abel must somehow have fired, after all. Without a gun?

"Another boat," Abel said, and in a moment the boat itself appeared, not forty feet away, rowing towards us.

"They fell together. Right in here," a man's voice said. "There's one. There they both are."

We watched with envy while they poled their boat, forcing it into the lily pads, and picked up the ducks.

"What kind are they?" Abel called.

"Woodies," one of the men called back, and they rowed

[38]

away again. It was light enough to see the outline of their boat when they stopped, now that we knew how to look for it.

"We'll move over," Abel said. "Could you get the anchor up, Perk?"

Abel rowed us twenty yards farther from the boat which had shot the wood ducks. Then we waited for a long time, it got lighter and lighter and the fog thinner, and Abel told us what the woodies indicated.

"Means there's no sign to think there are any Northern ducks come in yet," he said. "Wood ducks breed right here. Guess they do all over the country, don't they?"

He was asking the bird-watcher who had recently failed to identify a heron in flight; Abel was a nice boy. I told him what little I could remember from reading—I know a good deal more about wood ducks now.

There is a wry fatefulness about one's having been the first duck I ever saw shot, for they have haunted my Iowa openings since I came here. They are a small, beautifully marked duck, hunted almost to extinction before protective laws came in because their plumage was so valued for trimming hats.

I saw my first pair close to a little later on that Florida morning. The fog had cleared, there was no sign of ducks in the air; Abel was in the bow, now, Perk in the center with his bottle breached, when the men in the other boat came rowing past, heading for water open enough to start their motor.

I asked if I might see the ducks, and they obligingly stopped rowing and held the pair up.

"Pretty things," Perk said. "God they're pretty."

"Give most anything to know where the roost is," said one man.

"Yeh, bo," said the other. "Have us some duck-ee shooting."

The remark stayed in my mind as a puzzle for several years; here in Iowa I learned what it meant. A flock of wood ducks, which may include a hundred birds or more, does seem to have a regular roosting place—a little slough, some wooded marsh—from which they fly out to feed first thing each morning, to which they will return at an easily predictable time, just after sundown. Since not even being shot at seems to shake their regularity, they are pretty easy marks for the gunner who has located a roost, especially in the evening when they come in tired and careless, trusting apparently that once the roost is reached they will be safe. A hunter waiting there in the gathering darkness need hardly be concealed. Their flight is relatively slow, their outline, if the situation requires that one distinguish them, as close to unmistakable as any duck's in flight can be. Wood ducks needed a lot of protecting, but they are back on the game list now, in any case, in a limited way; in Iowa most years we are generally permitted to include one (but no more than one) in a day's bag.

I don't know what the legal status was in Florida that year, but the men in the boat certainly showed no sign of discarding their wood ducks as they moved off. It was not more than a few minutes after that, six-thirty and a beautifully clear day, when Abel said:

"Well. What do you all want to do?"

"I want to have a drink," said Perk, who already had. "You duck hunters ready for a drink?"

I hated to refuse; I had a lot of fellow feeling for Perk now. But I thought the lead was Abel's.

"There might be a duck come by," Abel said, speaking past Perk to me, but he said it doubtfully. "Sometimes they keep moving around—maybe some wind'll come up to move them."

"Let's stay then," I said.

"Well, then . . . you care if I *do* have a drink?" Abel, it seemed, felt the lead was mine. He hadn't used the term "sir," but it was in his voice, and it was then I began to see what a parody my education as a hunter might be of the customary one, which involves an older man and a boy—starting then, and often afterwards there was someone much younger than myself instructing me. Boys made good teachers; they were so sure of what they knew—and not until the situation took some sort of turn would I be reminded who the older man was.

"My God," I said, "let's pass that jug."

We sat there in the growing brightness, passing the bottle back and forth, watching the other boats leave the lake, one by one. Each time a boat started we'd promise ourselves some ducks would be put up and fly our way, but it never happened. It began to get hot, the liquor tasted marvelously strong and felt fine inside so early in the day—I was reluctant to share the sandwiches which Abel passed around, at first. Then I was ravenous and ate more than anyone. Inside the boat things passed from congenial to giddy, and there should have been a schoolmaster to take those loaded guns away. I don't recall which of us started shooting at blackbirds but soon enough we were all at it, and laughing as we missed, and I do remember one I hit with a wildly lucky shot—I remember how he folded his wings and hit the water head first, like a diver. I insisted on trying to retrieve him, and when all the shells were gone, about seven dollars' worth blasted hilariously and irresponsibly into the air, we did paddle over there; but the bird had drifted out of sight by then.

In all the yelling and shooting we managed to finish Perk's bottle, and even to decide that it was time to go back. I wasn't going to let those college kids treat me like I was pappy-aged, either, so when it came time to fasten the outboard back onto the transom, I wrestled it up off the floor by myself, and heaved it right past Abel's waiting hands, across Perk's solid lap, and over the side of the boat. It gasped and bubbled like a live thing going down.

"I'll get it," I cried, knowing the water wasn't more than waist deep, and jumped after it; beat Abel into the water because he stopped to take his shoes off, and old Perk cried, "Wait for me," and joined us.

There was enough mud on the bottom so that the water actually came to my chest by the time I settled. I could kick the motor, but when I tried to duck under and grasp it, I'd lose my footing. We needed someone Perk's size for the job; the only trouble was that when, between the three of us, gasping and ducking and still full of laughter at the mishap, we got our motor raised, the boat had drifted away unnoticed down the canal.

Getting it back cost Abel a pair of pants, which he removed to enable himself to swim better. We simply couldn't find the sunken pants again, any more than we could my right shoe which pulled off in the mud. And any duck hunter knows what happened when we were finally clambering back into the boat, wringing out clothes, putting the motor back on, knowing it probably wouldn't start without being taken apart and cleaned.

Perk was lighting a cigarette, and had just finished saying to Abel, "I hear you're a real rowing champ," and Abel'd replied, wringing out his shirt:

"No, not me Perk. But I'll be glad to watch you and learn."

And I'd laid down my gun to reach for the oars.

It was then two ducks came by, low and easy right across the stern.

I need only think of myself that day, shooting wantonly, getting drunk, releasing tensions I hardly understood in a stream of actions more childish than a child's common sense would permit, to understand the behavior, on the whole less conspicuously stupid, of the men I see out here on opening days. They shoot high birds, do not know one duck from another, crowd too close together and let cripples swim away to die—but on the whole are careful with their guns and educate more birds through fear than they actually hurt. Many of them are able to hunt only once or twice a year. They come out opening day from the cities as a matter of ritual, and we will see them perhaps once more, some Saturday or Sunday during the season. My circumstances are different; I live in the country and can adjust my hours. I can establish a pattern of devotions, going to bed when the children do, getting up before dawn daily, that permits me to hunt the best hours of every morning before work, or of the afternoon if I decide to work early. I have been able to go hunting (not always effectively, of course) several hundred times by now.

Why can't I leave opening day to the others, if it alienates me from them? I never could. I am not a man of many longings—longing after all is a product of melancholy, melancholy a product of disoccupation, and I keep busy. Yet, like anyone I suppose, I sometimes feel that immemorial emptiness, and at those times it seems to me I live ten months each year to reach the two when I may take a gun and go out to the woods again, and the riverbank, in my old fantasy of being one to one with nature. When finally the law permits this, another day has always been too long to wait.

There have been times, you see—eight or ten out of the hundreds, and their memory is what pulls me back so—when the fantasy has been exceeded. Let me recall one, for if I cannot make the pleasure clear, my strength of feeling will seem inane.

In the first of my Iowa duck seasons, still learning, I hunted with a young New Englander, recently transplanted here like myself, named Henry Akers. Among the pieces of equipment that I bought were a duck call and a record of instructions for calling mallards. Mallards are the ducks which are at the same time most common and most choice in this flyway—large, strong, fairly wary, and exceptionally good to eat; there are hunters here who will shoot nothing else. The analogous duck on the Atlantic flyway is the black duck which, Henry claimed, was even warier; calling, in New England where he had hunted all his life, would be worse than a waste of time, would warn black ducks away. Because of this, my intention of calling mallards made him uneasy ("Hell! mallards and blacks are first cousins"); he approved my practicing with the record, or with the half-tame ducks which spent the fall in a pond in the town park ("Damn it, they're swimming towards us, aren't they, Henry?"), but in actual hunting situations, I could only try my call when I went out alone.

One morning, by myself on the Iowa river sandbar off which our decoys floated, I called to a single which was coming down the river, and it seemed to me she responded, pausing in the air with her wings cupped, over the decoys. It was an easy shot and I got her, a huge hen mallard, biggest duck I'd seen that season. Henry would have said that she was coming in to the decoys anyway, in spite of the calling; I'd have replied that, anyway, the calling didn't scare her off.

As a matter of fact, that is pretty much what Henry said and I replied, the same evening at a cocktail party. (I am too much of a spook about early rising to go to evening parties during duck season.) It was one of those parties that goes on

[43]

past cocktail time, and one of those at which someone finds the
host's tape-recorder; into this machine, with piano and bongo-
drum accompaniment, I was persuaded to play a chorus of
"Georgia on My Mind" on the duck call: Quack-quack/Quack-
quack/Qua', qua', qua', quack—Henry, on his ninth martini,
said the intonation and the passion were there, now, to bring
the mallards up out of the sloughs. When I left, at eight-thirty,
he was on his tenth martini and willing to endorse any amount
of duck calling I might want to plan for morning. I did, it's
true, have to remind him of the dispensation when I picked
him up, a little before five next morning—he was pretty blear
of eye and in no mood for bright debate.

We were on our sandbar, hidden in clumps of short willows, when I saw ducks in the air—mallards, I thought, but
they are not all that easy to tell at two hundred yards. They
were way out, over trees across the river, a flock of thirty and
moving fast.

"Go ahead and try them," Henry whispered. "What can
we lose? They're paying us no attention, and they'll be gone
in a minute."

I blew a greeting call, loud and strong. As far as I could
tell, the ducks kept right on down the river without missing
a stroke. I raised the pitch and blew the come-back call. They
disappeared. But Henry said:

"They swung. I think they swung towards us, just before
they went out of sight."

So I kept on calling to the open sky, and our ducks
reappeared, making a circle over the river below us before
they went out of sight again, with me blowing the come-back
call insistent as I could.

"Too bad," Henry said. "You swung them anyway."

I set myself to watch up river again. Henry was watching
down. And suddenly there was a loud wind behind us, a sound
like swaying branches and loose leaves, and I looked up, there
wasn't time to look back. Above me, over each shoulder and
all around, the thirty ducks were dropping in, falling across
my vision in a splendid flurry, gleaming in the sun as they slid
towards the decoys in front of us. Oh, that was a moment,
even if my gun did seem to fire by itself, both barrels without

[44]

raising a feather, a spontaneous salute, not an attack, as if the gun, too, (an extension of myself, an extra limb) shared my astonishment and awe. I don't believe I even had it to my shoulder, for the locking flange behind the breech jumped back with the recoil and opened the tip of my right thumb quite painfully. Bleary-eyed, inefficient, hungover Henry shot a double—he tried to say that one was mine, but I knew worse.

But I had tears in my eyes—not from missing the shot, not because my thumb hurt—they were tears of wonder that I could call up such a sight, all those ducks filling the air, shining and dropping like snowflakes all around my head.

ii.

There was once a decent opening on ducks, too, a fine one —one to which I doubt any other first day ever will compare. It is curiously apposite to my last anecdote, for it, too, involves musical rendition and calling to birds.

It was in 1961, and it's odd that it should have been good, for the tension of waiting was greater for me, as summer passed slowly along towards fall that year, than ever before. The previous October I'd been in South America—but it got to be spring down there in late November, nesting season; shooting wasn't against the law, only the grain, and when I dressed out a female one day and found eggs inside, I quit hunting. After that it seemed to me that I waited a long time.

About the first of August in the year I got back, I met Brian. He is an amateur trumpeter, a good deal better one than I, and we met playing in somebody's cellar. Blows there a man with lip so dead that he can't cut me on the trumpet? I've never found him, and certainly not Brian, whose lip— very-stiff-upper, or British Canadian variety—was astonishing on the high solos. If his playing seemed a little inhibited, relying more on phrases remembered than passages invented, it was pretty much in character—he was a thin, fluent, conventionally good-looking young man, but somewhat stiff in manner. Anyway, he had a characteristic that made me happier to meet him at that moment, in my circumstances, than any other trumpeter in history. Was Bix born in Canada? Or Louis? Bunny? Miles?

[45]

I had been pondering those ducks up there, trading back and forth at the head of the flyway, not due to start down until October or even November, and all that prevented me from going up among them, as soon as it might be legal, was the lack of a companion who would know some of the right localities.

During the whiskey break between "Basin Street" and "Cherry," I remarked to Brian, with all the casualness of a man asking if you happen to have a spare pipe of opium around the house, that he must be looking forward to the duck opening up his way in just a few weeks. Brian said he really wasn't much of a duck hunter. I waggled a finger and spoke an owlish obscenity at him for such unbecoming modesty. Brian admitted politely that it might be fun to try the early shooting some time, and as the pianist sat down to play an introduction ("My Funny Valentine"; Brian's choice), I accepted him into it. I suspect he couldn't think of a courteous way to back off that would go fast enough to let him listen to the chords. It was clear that my pressing distressed him though—he could barely get away from the melody when his chorus came, on the tune he'd picked himself, but when it was my turn I actually did quite well (at least Carrot Appleson, who plays guitar, didn't suggest for once that I might like to try another one on the duck call).

Brian kept trying to make it clear, in the next week or so when I'd see or call him, that he was a fisherman, not a hunter —an easterner, from Ontario. The great Canadian duck-breeding grounds are in Saskatchewan and Manitoba, as far from the lakes where Brian grew up as North Dakota is from Albany. He turned out to be the first person I ever hunted with who looked to me for instruction, rather than the other way around. I think I could say I was a journeyman duck hunter by then, a classification which I doubt I'll ever manage to exceed, and reliable enough in basic techniques.

Manitoba seemed to be the place for us, being the closer of the two provinces, and we learned by correspondence that there would indeed be an opening to fit the time we had available, which was an eight-day week, starting August

27th and ending on September 3rd. At noon on September 1st shooting would begin, not in the whole province but in the northernmost part, and I guess I might have let Brian off had not his enthusiasm for the trip increased so remarkably when we learned about it.

"Flinflan," he said, naming the town where the road north ends. From the map we had, it seemed to be just a few miles south of the fifty-fifth parallel which we would have to cross in order to hunt legally September 1st. "Boy, look at it. We'll have to get North of Flinflan!" *North* had so much meaning for him that his voice couldn't really hold the word steady. It stood, I began to learn, for a whole mystique, something more than *frontier* though that was certainly part of it. The rest, for a young Canadian, was: away from the border, away from Yankeeness. When you gave in to *south,* it meant working for Ford or BBD&O or Coca Cola, or, worse in a way, for some Canadian firm formed in their image. *North* has always been where a man might find Canadian identity, distinct, national, unsoiled.

We had a rough enough time getting north to satisfy anybody's mystique, though the rigors were not those imposed by weather and terrain so much as by fanbelts, generators, and small-town filling stations, all of which seemed to close firmly at six P.M. Our plan had been to make Flinflan in two days of nonstop driving; by midnight of the second day we had barely arrived at the southern town of Grand Portage, just west of Winnipeg. On the third day, when we'd meant to be outfitting in Flinflan, scouting out the trails and lumbering roads we assumed must lead north from it in order to get across the parallel, we had to turn back to Winnipeg to replace a tire. On the fourth day, August 30th (we should have been setting up camp, spotting birds and passes, building a blind), we were still finishing the first leg, heavy-eyed, grimy, even a little feverish from the excitement of having passed, at dawn, a roadside lake unimaginably crowded with teal and shovelers. It was evening when we finally drove into Flinflan, and there we got a harder jolt than the one we took when the tire blew— the early opening wasn't meant for people just north of Flinflan at all. It was meant for people even more remote, hundreds of miles east and a little north in Manitoba, the Eskimos and Indians of Hudson's Bay. You could go back to a town called The Pas, and take the train from there to Hudson's Bay if you had the time and the price. We didn't.

"Still, it's legal to hunt anywhere north of the 55th parallel," Brian said. We were in a restaurant, straining over a large-scale map, trying to figure the thing out. "That's only thirty miles from here."

"There's got to be a way up," I said. But there was only water, rock, forest, muskeg, and winter roads. Muskeg is a ground cover of moss several feet thick, with moisture underneath; winter roads are suggested trails across lakes, after they freeze. "There's got to be."

"Not by car," said Brian, who'd seen muskeg before.

The fifth day was frantic. We had driven back down from Flinflan the night before, to a fork in the road, and slept there a couple of hours. Then we woke and started north again, on the east fork, towards a town called Snow Lake, even closer to the parallel, seven impenetrable miles south of the line. But you couldn't tell us it was impenetrable; perhaps we were a little hysterical by then, for we drove through and out of town; hid boat, car, decoys, and all the gear we'd brought along in the woods; and started to hike north without a trail, carrying guns, sleeping bags, and what food we could manage. We'd walked half an hour or so before we began to realize how foolish we were being—going in, no compass, relying on the map, the sun position and our watches, towards some unknown point in the forest, as if merely to step across the beckoning, imaginary line called fifty-five would provide that we'd arrive at a place where ducks were.

I had just stepped into a hole in the muskeg and got some water in my boot—we were approaching yet another pond which we'd have to skirt. As I sat down to empty the boot, I said to Brian:

"Damn, boy. I don't know about this."

"I was thinking the same thing," Brian said. "You've got a wife and children."

I don't know too many people who could say a thing like that seriously, but it was all right coming from him—unsenti-

[48]

mental, a statement of considered fact. "Are you lost?" I asked.

"I don't think so, yet," he said. "But that pond looks just like the other two. And none of them is big enough to be on the map."

"No ducks, either," I said. "I don't think there's anything out in here but squirrels and jays, and not many of them. Let's go back."

It took us a little over two hours to find the car.

Snow Lake is a mining town, but there are still a few of the trappers and fishermen left around who established it, living in shanties away from the mining-company houses, the new stores and school. We spent the evening of the fifth day, August 31st, in bars and restaurants, talking to whomever we could. Generally, it surprised the men we spoke with to think that legal duck hunting could start tomorrow so close at hand; generally they thought this an interesting enough curiosity, but quite impossible to take advantage of. But finally, near closing time, we found the old man one would have to find in such a situation, who could tell us of a long, narrow lake, and a car track leading to it made by old-time commercial fishermen. If we drove there, to the southern end, and put our duck boat in, the outboard motor could take us the eleven miles, up across the fifty-fifth, to where the lake grew shallow and drained into a grassy river. And he had heard that sometimes, long years past, men found ducks there, but had never been himself.

It was our only chance and we took it, following his directions as best we could by headlight through the woods, camping finally, pretty sure this must be it, at the tip of the lake the old man had called Little Jerry.

We were up again early, too impatient to stay in our bags and get the sleep we both needed by then, consumed with the idea of being across the parallel before noon, the appointed, artificial hour.

"We'll hunt this afternoon."

"Sleep up there?" Brian asked.

"Sure. And hunt again in the morning, rush back down the lake, throw the ducks in the car and take off for home."

"How many ducks?" Brian asked.

"Twenty, if this is really it, and they're really there. And we can get them."

We were too far gone to laugh at ourselves, and we were right about one thing: we had stumbled on Little Jerry. As we started out of the bay in the little aluminum boat, onto the lake itself, even I, unused to maps of water and shoreline, could see that this lake corresponded. Brian, doing something familiar at last, took us along with real confidence, and we were lost on the water only once. It was the worst moment of a trip which had had more than its share of bad ones. One inlet, one island, one bay, on water like that, where the vegetation on shore never changes and there are no buildings, no clearings, looks just like any other. Brian, counting dots and guessing shapes and distance on the map, got us a long way correctly, four or five miles I'd guess, before he took us around a long island and into the wrong arm of the lake, and as we went along it, unsuspecting, past loons and shore birds, we saw a hideous thing: we saw a tower, way off on a ridge to the west. There we were, six days north and out on a lake where no one had been for years, getting more and more remote—and there was that wretched structure—Berlin, Formosa, Cuba—part of the early warning system I suppose.

"I don't care if we're right or wrong," Brian said. "That goddamn thing isn't on the map, too new I guess, but even if it's where we're supposed to be, I don't want to hunt under it, do you?"

"No," I said. "That isn't what I came for," and I turned the boat around. It was good I did. We went back around the long island, then around another, and saw the entrance to a narrow fjord-like passage with steep banks.

"There's the arm that goes north," Brian said. "It's got to be." And he was right.

It took us nearly two hours to go up it, but gradually they became happy ones. As we got surer and surer of our course and direction, we passed the mouth of a stream which showed up clearly on the map. ("It's this one," Brian said. "Because we've just gone by this bay, here, with the marsh just after it. Half a mile, and we'll be across the fifty-fifth.")

[50]

We crossed, or so we figured, at 11:15. At about 11:40 the banks began to level out, marsh grass showed on both sides. Then the grass began showing underneath us, and at 11:50 we could see bottom. I stopped the motor, there was that hush that comes with cutting a noisy outboard that's been running so long you're accustomed to it, and then Brian said, very quietly:

"It's the grassy river." It was a beautiful place; the grass moved gently on both sides of us in the slight current of flowing water. Beyond the grass were open woods rolling very gradually upwards, and an area, down river, that seemed meadowy. It was a windless, sunny noon, and completely quiet, until, so close to noon it seemed uncanny, there came, from around the river bend towards which we drifted, a sound, like a chorus of high-voiced men saying *Brrrrr*, rolling the *R*'s.

"That ought to be 'quack,' shouldn't it?" Brian whispered, and I smiled.

"Divers," I whispered back, feeling the smile become a grin. "That's the feed call of diving ducks. Let's get set."

We had a camouflage net which fit over ourselves and the boat, with openings for our heads and arms and shoulders. I tipped the motor up, and we draped the net on, putting on hooded jackets of the same material.

"Turn around," I whispered. Brian was in the bow, facing backwards. He turned front, his shotgun cradled in his arms, and I moved into the rowing seat but facing forward, too, so that I rowed with a pushing stroke but could see where we were going. Thus we moved around the bend.

The ducks came in sight farther down than I'd imagined, from the noise they were making, two hundred yards about— fifty or sixty of them. I held my breath when I saw them, foolishly enough, but perhaps we both did.

"What kind?" Brian looked back at me. "They're black and white."

I shipped oars and looked down through the binoculars. "Buffleheads," I said. "I'll keep us moving towards them. I don't know if they'll let us get in range—it'll probably be long and sporty shooting."

I rowed as quietly as I could, watching the flock for signs

[51]

of alarm. These were eight or ten broods, probably, feeding and diving together, which had hatched out and matured right here, and because we had come a long, hard way to find them, I watched with real delight. But by the time I had cut the distance to seventy or eighty yards, I was tense again with all kinds of things—the one I focused on was Brian: he would shoot too soon. He would shoot them on the water. Somehow he'd spoil it. He shouldered his gun; we were fifty yards away now, and I wanted to yell, "Not yet, not yet"—and, "Let them fly, please let them fly"—but perhaps he knew. I hunched under the net. Some of the buffleheads were shifting now, as they swam, watching us—but most continued just to swim about, sunning, feeding. We crept within forty yards, a possible shot now, difficult of course from a boat but . . . Thirty yards. I don't know which I was watching harder, for the ducks to get up, spanking across the water as divers do and exploding into the air together—or for Brian's right shoulder to move forward, shoving the gunstock tight against his cheek to take the sitting shot I feared, but didn't feel I could deny him. The ducks were quiet; twenty yards. One dived; another after it. The shoulder relaxed.

"Well, for God's sake," Brian said. "Look." And he began to laugh and point. Over at the left one of the little drake buffleheads was moving, swimming right towards us to look us over.

"Hey duck," I said, laying down the oars. "That's not fair."

"Come on," said Brian. "How about a little flying."

The drake kept coming, brighteyed, and bobbed to a stop hardly an oar's length away.

"Hey, bufflehead," I said. "Look, will you get your boys together and take off?"

"Get a buffle on," yelled Brian, and with that the drake began to bob away, his curiosity apparently satisfied, but two others now came towards us. "You silly, tame birds."

"What we need on this duck hunt's some women and children and a bag of bread crusts."

"Now what do we do?" Brian was grinning about as happily as I ever saw anybody grin.

[52]

"Maybe we can find some fliers in another group," I said. We began rowing around. There were little groups of buffleheads all along the shore, and we found we could get them to move away from us if we splashed hard enough with the oars, but they only swam, till they were forty yards or so away; then they'd stop again to eat. When I fired an experimental shot up into the air, hoping to startle some up into flight for Brian that way, one or two swam farther; the majority simply dived.

But if the shot didn't fly the buffleheads, it did put up some other divers, in a little bay across the river. They got up and flew around quite smartly over there, before settling down in more or less the same place, and I made them out, when they were back on the water, as either scaup, lesser scaup, or ring-necks. The three species are pretty close in appearance.

We poled over there; it had got too weedy to row. They were a good deal more nervous than the buffleheads, but not much more inclined towards flight. They swam, generally, before we were quite in range—first of one bunch, then another and another. Finally, though, we pushed a pair into a little indentation, and they did fly up and wheel out over the shore. In the unsteady boat, which I had to try to swing so that he could turn with the direction of their flight, and given his lack of experience, Brian did the understandable thing; he fired twice, missing completely and whooping after each shot.

"I told you I was a duffer," he said. "I've pot-shot ducks, but I never yet hit one flying, even from dry land."

"I pot-shot one once. It gave me bad dreams for a week," I said.

"Let's trade," said Brian. "Have a good dream."

We traded places, he poled me after some ducks, one went up, and it was my turn to miss—but I didn't. I hit, a lovely crossing shot from left to right, and the bird was dead in the air. Brian rowed us over to pick her up, a fat little female lesser scaup.

"Take some more," Brian said. "That was great."

"Your turn."

"No. Go ahead. I'll pole."

"Thanks," I said, and then with one of those easy insights

one sometimes has with a friend: "Hey. You don't really want to shoot one, do you?"

"Not any more." He was holding my duck. "I wouldn't trade her, or have her alive again for anything. And I want to see you get nineteen others; but I'll pole."

"I'm with you," I said. "Who could feel like a hunter with ducks like these?" What I felt more like was a visitor who'd done something rude in the living room, and been forgiven.

"All-ee, all-ee in-free," Brian called to the ducks. "You come barreling down the flyway in a couple of weeks, and come over my blind, it may be different." Man can kill anything, if he sets his mind to it—man can spare all the life he wants to, just as well.

We went back down the lake that afternoon. We trolled a little, without luck, stopped at a weed-bed to cast, and caught northern pike. We kept one for supper, a relatively small one, and he made a marvelous fish course by the fire on which our single scaup was roasting. We opened all sorts of canned delicacies we'd had no time for up to then. We ate for hours, it seemed, and the duck was the finest we ever tasted; I suppose that follows. Then, just after dusk, we crawled into our sleeping bags, there at the foot of the lake, the bags lying on moss, and we had glasses of Canadian whiskey in our hands and loons to listen to. I don't think either of us felt that he was tired, but Brian was talking about something—a particularly big pike he'd caught once, I believe it was—and went to sleep in the middle of a sentence. I thought I'd just lie there and finish my whiskey and watch the stars come out, but I never saw the first one.

We were up at dawn, washing and swimming in the cool lake water, when a great flight of birds appeared, very high, coming down the lake towards us, huge birds against the mottled sky in a flight of several hundred. We looked, standing to our waists in water, and tried to call them geese, but their honking, as they came closer, was nothing like the geese I'd heard. It was rather like loon cries but with extraordinary volume, more defiant in its first notes and trailing off into a throbbing, drawn-out tremolo.

"Are they cormorants?" Brian suggested. They were near the head of our bay now.

"No, much bigger," I said. "And slimmer. With their legs trailing, like herons." The leaders were nearly overhead, so that I could see the outlines clearly. "But their heads stick out."

" 'The air full of flying crosses,' " Brian quoted suddenly, remembering, as he told me later, a tag from his childhood. "Sandhill cranes."

They seemed to sail as much as fly, and we stood naked in the water looking up, listening; then Brian said:

"I can play that call." And he ran out of the water and over to the car, where he got our trumpet cases. We'd brought the horns along with some idea of practicing, to keep in shape; but hadn't had them out, of course.

I left the water, and went towards where Brian was sitting on the beach, picking up a towel to dry myself. He was putting his mouthpiece in; he pointed the bell up in the air.

"Come on," he said, and I went over and opened my case, too. He played an imitation of the call the cranes were sounding, softly twice, and then full volume. It was pretty close, though the birds neither slowed nor speeded up. He turned it into a simple phrase of melody, and I noticed that the loon, out on the bay, turned to look but without alarm.

I sat then, and took out my own trumpet. The sun was halfway up, and the cranes glistened as they caught it. I held my trumpet ready and watched Brian, naked, with water drying on his thin shoulder blades in the sunrise, playing to the passing cranes, playing to the last of them, playing as they disappeared—to the loon, to the shorebirds, to the lake—with effortless, lyric elaborations. Quietly as I could, I put my horn away. It was Brian's Song of the North, and I didn't feel I had a chorus coming.

iii.

Here is a characteristic Iowa opening; it took place later the same year. It has a cast of four, besides myself: My Wife, The Two Brothers, and Genghis Khan.

I say each year, of openings, that if I go at all, it will be all alone and to a place so remote it will take bloodhounds to find me. I was saying this, as a matter of fact, to Genghis Khan over the telephone one day, about a week before the opening, and he replied:

"That's okay. I don't mind covering some ground with you."

"No," I said. "No, if I take anybody, I ought to take my wife. And she's not experienced enough to enjoy hunting with others around."

Just as I began that sentence a vacuum cleaner switched off, and as I hung up the voice of a pleased woman said:

"Really? Are you taking me opening day?"

Genghis Khan, a faculty colleague at the university where I teach, is one of the people who, having proposed a meeting and had it refused, must continue proposing others until one is agreed to. He called back almost immediately; he was convinced that I knew where ducks were and, as a matter of fact, he was right—as I have said, I am out and around them all year long. For more than a week I'd been keeping hunting hours and visiting in turn the dozen different places where I'd do my duck hunting—sloughs, sandbars, a small lake, two big marshes, and a number of pot holes, all on land which is open to public hunting.

I was in debt to Genghis Khan for a hunting favor—he had shown me some good squirrel woods the year before. Now he proposed to join me on one of the scouting trips he knew I made, and I didn't see how I could refuse.

Meanwhile, the Two Brothers had entered my preparations. They were a couple of polite and personable Southerners who had come to study in our graduate school, and they paid a call to ask if I'd consent to give them some general information about goose hunting in the area—goose season had opened the week before. I tried to tell them that local goose hunting didn't amount to much, but they took this as one of those disclaimers made as a matter of propriety or perhaps proprietariness—I told them what I knew about places along the river and forgot it.

Here is how things worked out: On Wednesday, before

the Saturday noon opening, Genghis Khan got out of bed in time to join me for a look at a marsh where I'd been seeing teal. There were no teal that day but, in a small open-water area, at the end I hadn't visited before, were about fifteen mallards—there were trees enough and marsh grass so that we could work our way quite close to them. It was just the sort of place I'd have picked to start the season in solitude, but I had boxed myself off—the Khan shared rights of discovery to it now; anyway, it would have been pretty muddy going for my wife.

That afternoon the two brothers showed up to close the lid of the box: they were quite discouraged. They had conscientiously followed out all my offhand suggestions about goose hunting, and seen no sign of geese. They were respectful and pleasant, but I could tell they felt I'd misled them. Misleading is a kind of minor sport to some sportsmen; though it is not one of my pleasures to direct a stranger to the part of a trout stream I know to be unstocked, or away from a field where pheasants rest, I have often enough been the game in that aspect of the chase. I had left Moon, my larger dog, behind that morning, not wanting him to run up ducks if we should find some; he needed exercise, and I was preparing to go out again.

"Why don't you come along if you have time?" I said. "I'll show you a couple of duck places anyway."

I figured I could give another place away and still have plenty left to hunt—and they did have time. Their names were George and Fred.

The place I took them to is about a mile off the Iowa river. There are two big sloughs there, first a round shallow one bordered by willow trees, then a deep narrow one which winds through the woods for three hundred yards or so and is fairly well hidden. There is also a puddle of shallow water in the middle of a field beyond the sloughs. I decided to show the two brothers the round slough and the puddle; I didn't want to show anybody the long slough. It was a wood-duck roost.

I hadn't expected much waterfowl activity in the full light of afternoon, but I was quite mistaken. We had gone no more than sixty yards from the road, walking the edge of the round

[57]

slough, before Moon jumped a pair of pintails who went noisily off, and in so doing warned a little bunch of teal we hadn't seen, which joined the big ducks in the air.

"Looks like quite a place," Fred said.

We angled away from the round slough, towards the puddle, and as we crossed the open field yet another duck went by us, going to the same place we were. We got to the puddle and there he was, a green-winged teal swimming around busily; green wings are rather uncommon here, and I was delighted to see one close. The teal didn't seem to notice us. I collared the dog and made him sit with us under the only tree near the puddle, to watch if ducks would come and go.

"Too bad it's so open," George said.

"Wouldn't take much to dig a trench—over there on the east side, where the grass is long?" Fred pointed. "There's a log we could drop along the back edge to sit on, and there's plenty of brush to pile around it."

"Carry out a couple of boards for the bottom," George said, nodding. "Keep our feet out of the mud."

Two more green-winged teal came over just then, started to skid down to join the first, saw us, flared, and went away, calling the other away with them.

"You're welcome to the place," I said, and that set off a complicated argument, consisting of the following elements: I was reluctant to insist too strongly that I wouldn't want to open the season here myself, for fear of its sounding as if I were concealing even better places, which wasn't really so. Moreover, this particular puddle, which I hadn't been considering particularly, would be a pleasant place for my wife, easy to get to, good promise of there being ducks to shoot at— and the kind of blind they were talking of building would be a lot more comfortable than one which I might improvise for her. On their part, the argument was based on a conviction that I must certainly have intended hunting here; if I'd rather that they found another place, they certainly would—they couldn't possibly agree to using this one by themselves.

It is much more difficult to refuse a courteous stranger than a friend, but what finally decided me was an entirely selfish consideration: green-winged teal came here. I had never shot one and knew of no others in the area. By the time we got up to go back I had told myself that opening day would be a mess in whatever accessible place we hunted; that common politeness now required that the two brothers be included; that my wife would enjoy their easy Southern sociability (as well as the tidy blind they planned); that if we didn't join them, we could expect to be joined elsewhere by people we didn't know; that now I would have a genuine reason for turning down yet another man I had been fearing to hear from— with these and other supports, ramshackle buttresses for a building I hadn't intended making, I accepted.

So it was arranged, and on Saturday morning while I was loading boots and tools in the car so that I could go help work on the blind, driving in to confront me with my deceit (though of course he didn't know it) came Genghis Khan in a red Corvair sedan.

"When are we going to get those mallards?" he demanded.

"Well, I told you. I'm taking my wife today."

"To the marsh? The marsh you mean?"

"No, we'll be someplace else. Couldn't you and I go back to the marsh tomorrow?" I had been past the marsh early that morning, and knew the birds were still there.

"Someone else might get them today."

He was on the edge of indignation; I was on the edge of guilt and lost my footing. "Okay," I said. "I'm going out to work on a blind now. I'll be there with my wife at noon. Look, a few minutes after the opening, I'll leave her for a little while and come join you. Okay?"

The brothers and I made a pretty nice little blind, log seat and board floor as advertised, poles at the corners, wire between them, and quantities of artful brush piled on. The concealment was fine, the visibility good to all sides. At eleven-thirty my wife joined us, coming across the field with thermos and sandwiches. So far no one else was trying to hunt our puddle, though one man came over and watched us for a while. I saw half a dozen go in to take cover around the round slough, and at least two going down to the long one where the wood ducks were. I found myself hoping that there'd be a warden

[59]

working in the area—one wood duck in the limit was all that
was legal. It was a poor year, and the total limit was just two
ducks a day, four in possession, and a season of thirty days.
There isn't really any agreeable way, to my mind, of
shooting from a blind with four people in it, but we made the
best plan we could—we agreed to shoot in pairs, two sitting
back each time ducks came in. The brothers insisted that my
wife and I stand first and that is what we were doing at noon,
our decoys out in the puddle, and stakes showing above its
surface at twenty, thirty, and forty yards.

George was watching his wrist and just as he said, "Now.
Season's open," a small duck bolted in from the left rear, right
on cue. I glanced at my wife, wanting her to take it—she was
still loading her gun. I threw mine to my shoulder, late and
hurried, but sometimes an error like that is good for my shooting—I don't have time to remember to make my characteristic
mistakes. My gun went up and the duck down, from about six
feet above the water; skidded into the puddle and rolled over
dead, right by our thirty-yard stake. Two more ducks which
had been following far enough behind so we hadn't seen them
went into a maneuver which I always think of as a climbing
stop and headed towards the round slough at a height of
around two hundred yards.

The two brothers smiled, my wife frowned, and Moon
went straight out through the middle of the brush we'd spent
an hour arranging to retrieve the duck—a green-winged teal,
just what I wanted. As I looked at it the guns on the round
slough opened fire at the two specks in the sky, ten guns firing
harmlessly two or three times each.

"That's about three and a half dollars' worth of shotgun
shells," George said, and Fred said:
"Look out."

The noise on the round slough had put up three birds
which must have been hidden somewhere around its edge—
they must have jumped and caught all the men over there
temporarily unloaded. But our own performance was equally
sloppy; we were all four standing up gawking. What the ducks
saw was Fred and me squatting down, George and my wife
swinging shotguns at them. Like the ducks just before them,

they flared over the puddle and started to climb. It was a much harder shot than the one I'd made, and my wife missed with both barrels, though George got his. It was going so fast that its momentum carried it over the far side of the puddle where it fell in long grass—we'd have lost it without the dog, and his bill for damages to the blind was automatically withdrawn.

"Damn," George said, when he had it to look at. "A wood duck."

"You're allowed one this year."

"I know, but I should have known before I shot it. I got too excited."

My wife wanted to know *how* he could have known, and received three somewhat varying sets of directions for in-flight recognition, but it really isn't difficult, as she was willing to concede two or three hunts later last year: the wood duck carries its head in flight at an angle which makes it appear that it's looking downwards.

CONCEALMENT

"There was a woman down home once offered us ten dollars to bring her back a drake when shooting them was illegal," Fred said. "She wanted it to trim a hat."

"We were boys," George said. "And ten dollars was a lot of money—but I wish we hadn't done it. I'll never feel right about shooting one now."

"I find it hard to feel it's worse than no duck at all," said my empty-handed wife.

It was time, really, for me to excuse myself and go to meet Genghis Khan. I wanted a chance at one of those bright mallards we had spotted. What we'd planned was to crawl into range through the grass from two sides, having synchronized our watches first—then rise up together at an agreed second, jump the ducks, and hope they'd fly both ways. But I was reluctant to leave our blind before my wife had a bird, and I sat and watched for ten more minutes. That was as long as it took the two men who had heard our shots to reach the puddle from wherever they'd been. They walked, careful not to look at us, along the far edge of the puddle, taking their time, and then sat defiantly under the solitary tree.

"That's the end of the ducks till they get tired and leave," Fred said, and my wife gave me a nod which meant I might as well go keep my appointment. On the way to the road I met yet another man, wandering towards our puddle, but before we could exchange words there were some shots from the long slough and he changed course.

I drove towards the meeting place near the marsh which Genghis Khan and I had set, hoping I hadn't made him too impatient. It was false hope. The red sedan same roaring at me just after I'd turned into the right backroad, passed me going the other way, stopped and came roaring backwards. The window went down, the fearful face appeared and cried:

"Sorry. I owe you some mallards," and the red sedan plunged off again, leaving me less bewildered than I'd have liked. I had it all reconstructed long before that evening when he told me that he'd got itchy waiting, seen too many cars driving around looking for places, and decided to sneak the ducks by himself. Those opening-day ducks—when the

Great Khan rose up at the edge of their pool, they merely bunched up and quacked at him, and he let them have it on the water. Four with the first shot and three more with the second before they could get their wings going—that put him five over the limit and he was getting those birds home and out of sight with all possible speed. Yet he is quite a nice man, and a skillful hunter. Opening day.

Opening day. When I got back to the blind, the men were gone from under the tree. My wife had shot a wood duck, George a blue-winged teal, and some high-school boys, who had sneaked up without noticing the blind and unnoticed from it, a large hole in one of my decoys with a twenty-two rifle.

"You should have seen them jump up when Moon ran out and retrieved the decoy," George said.

"We were laughing too hard to be cross at Moon or the boys either," said my wife. "But I was scared at first. The bullet went just to the right of the blind. Fred went out and gave them hell."

"They tried to say they were squirrel hunting," George said, and Fred said he might as well spend his time giving boys hell for breaking laws—rifles are not permitted in waterfowl hunting—he certainly wasn't giving the ducks any. He'd had three chances and missed them all.

George, of course, had his two-bird limit now, and I was feeling a little as if the other duck in my limit, and my wife's as well, were traveling along the highway to Genghis Khan's house, whether we liked it or not. We stayed a while longer— long enough to see poor Fred lose another chance; he didn't even get to shoot. A small flight which looked like mallards appeared, George and I started to call to them, and immediately there was an unimaginable chorus of would-be quacking from the direction of the long slough. There were even a couple of honks mixed in.

"Some have their goose calls," George observed, as the mallards bolted.

"I walked over to that long slough while you were gone," Fred said. "There must be thirty men by now—all the ones who were on the round slough have gone there, and every time there's shooting or calling, two or three more go over. Like fishermen on a lake—somebody gets a fish and the boats rush at him from everywhere.''

I'd seen some snipe near the marsh, and my wife and I decided to go over and try for them. George said he'd stay with Fred, Fred said it was no use, nothing would come over and he couldn't hit it if it did. We all four left the blind in a mood of some depression. As soon as it was clear that we were leaving—in fact, while the two brothers and I were still wading around, picking up decoys—men started racing from two directions to take over our blind. We didn't stay to see who won.

On the road, where there were by now thirty or forty parked cars, the game warden was waiting to check the bags of people coming out, and I was pleased to see him. He observed that we were leaving rather early for a party that didn't have a full limit.

''It's pretty jammed up,'' I said, and the warden said there were other places that were even worse. I asked if he was finding many violations. I wouldn't have been too disappointed if he'd mentioned catching a man in a red sedan with seven mallards but he didn't.

''Just a few cases of two wood ducks instead of one,'' he said. ''And a man with a pied-billed grebe he thought was a diver—you'd think they'd know better than to carry them out and show them to me.''

Just then a pair of pintails went over our heads, very high, across the road and over towards the long slough. ''Listen, now,'' he said, and George estimated the cost of the shells we heard go off at ten dollars and fifty cents, and I said:

''Next year they can have opening day without me,'' but I didn't suppose I meant it.

November, 1962: I spoke more truly than I ever wished to. I did not hunt ducks on opening day this year—1962—nor have I on any day since, nor shall I tomorrow, or on any of the days remaining, though I am finding it difficult, some mornings, to sleep soundly through the dawn. I wake and see those visions of ten years ago sometimes—air full of ducks, ducks falling—and get up, perhaps to spite myself. Twice I have gone out to stand on a highway bridge, looking over the water, hearing a gun now and then, tugging my loose ends looser. It is hard to decide what to do with myself sometimes (but not often, for there is work; and there will be a pheasant season, and the dogs running) but it is my own fault: I am unwilling to abide by a majority decision or abet its sad results.

Six states, all of those, including mine, at the northern end of the Mississippi flyway, voted, at a meeting of the Flyway Council this year, to recommend to the Federal Bureau of Sport Fisheries and Wildlife, which sets the seasons, that there be no season. Eight states, the Southern block, voted in the face of knowledge and reason: with ducks down seventeen per cent from a bad year last year (I had seen limits go down in five years here from four ducks, to three, to two), the Southern states, where the great commercial duck-shooting enterprises are, voted that the season be extended and the bag limits increased. The Bureau, uneasy and theoretical, compromised. The season is neither closed nor extended: it is cut to twenty-five days. That is the compromise. The theoretical part comes in the provisions for this year's limit, which is once again two birds. But the Bureau seems to feel that duck hunters, unlike ornithologists who are capable of being puzzled over the species of a female duck passed from hand to hand among them (mallard? pintail? gadwall?), will be so discriminating as to observe the following provisions before deciding whether to shoot at a given bird:

It may not be a canvasback. It may not be a redhead. The season is closed on both. Only one wood duck is allowed, as before. Only one hooded merganser. (However, if it's an *American* merganser then extras are allowed, as are extra scaup—which need only be distinguished from ring-necks, an almost identical bird as noted, as they go by at forty miles an hour.) Finally, and worst: only one duck in the bag of two may be a black duck or a mallard.

"The condition of the mallard brook stock," says the Bureau, in a leaflet dated September 11, 1962, "is precarious. This year's breeding population was 30 per cent below 1961 ..." This is not very surprising, when connected with another report, from the South Dakota Conservation Digest: "To maintain adequate duck supplies, 2.1 young ducks must be produced for every adult bird . . . wing samples taken and analyzed for the 1961 season show that approximately four old mallards were killed for every young bird . . ." What will the wing samples show this year, if the breeding of the summer past produced a third fewer ducks?

Perhaps I could go out tomorrow, and not shoot a mallard, shoot some other kind of duck. But perhaps I couldn't—I have erred at times on wood ducks, which are so much easier. The Bureau has misplaced its confidence in me. Whatever the Southern vote, I will not trust myself to take the risk. And if I did, I would not want the placement of my car, my path through grass, my boot prints in the mud, or the sound of my gun to give away the places that I know, where ducks are. On whom should I rely, skilled hunter or not, to shoot within those exquisitely selective limits? Genghis Khan? There are a good many hunters like him. There are even more like that pathetic line of city men along the long slough last year. Here is what Fred told me, on the evening of that opening day, stopping by the house on his way into town:

"I've been back out," he said. "After leaving George, I just couldn't believe I was shooting so badly, so I went back out. First I was on the round slough, and I finally did get a duck. A strange little duck—a shoveler. Never saw one before. Then after a time I went over to the long slough, and it was like a battle. There were ducks coming in to roost, I guess, and there'd be a hundred shots every time one came down the line."

"I was afraid of that," I said. "I hoped maybe the warden's being there might stop it."

"You'd have had to have a warden for every hunter," Fred said. "You ought to see that slough. There wasn't a single dog among all those men, and the water's too deep to wade. So they didn't bother to retrieve the ones that fell in the water, and they're just floating around. But just about every man had his wood duck; I guess they kept expecting the next one to fall would be something else. Or maybe they knew— and knew the warden was waiting on the road. They just shot and shot, and . . . you want to go get yourself a wood duck? They're lying out there all over the bank."

3. The Goose Pits

I F ONE OF THE PEOPLE WHO OBJECT TO HUNTING
were to accuse me of relishing death, I would
have to admit that the most deeply felt moment
in wing shooting comes not with the flight of the bird nor with
its fall. The moment comes for me when, after missed shots
and missed opportunities, I hold at last the extraordinary
beauty, still almost alive, of a bird I have just killed. I wonder
if the whole wild patterning and color of Oriental ornament
wasn't learned from the red, white, lavender, and rose of a
cock pheasant, this exotically barred and whorled cousin of the
peacock now improbably at home in our cornfields. The forth-
right green head of the mallard drake, the softly mottled
breast of the duck, the formal delicacy of a bobwhite quail—
when my dog has offered such a prize to my hand, one of the
things that makes me a hunter is intensely satisfied. Is it envy?
I would not deny that envy is a part of it, for, among the
creatures, man, with his tottering two-legged stance, his flat
face and rudimentary fur, is no more one of the beautiful than
he is one of the powerful or the swift. Yet there is more to it,

I'd assert, than satisfied envy. There is a good deal of sadness, if not quite regret, and great love for the bird to haunt my triumph. None of the moments that hunting offers, when I hunt as I wish to, lacks complexity. But sometimes I find myself hunting as I wish not to, and then the moments can be simple enough. I am thinking now of a day three years ago, near Cairo, Illinois, when I hunched myself out of a pit I shared with three others to pick up a Canada goose that lay dead nearby. It had been in flight for five minutes since being hit the first time, by men in a pit a quarter of a mile away from ours, and had been hit at least once again in the interim before our guns ended its cripple's glide. It fell in mud, this specimen of the most magnificent race of North American waterfowl, and lay there drab and broken as I reached it. I was about as eager to pick it up and hold it as I might have been to pick up a barnyard goose, in thin condition and of mongrel breed, crushed by a car and lying on the shoulder of a modern road.

Let me assume that you are just as innocent of what Cairo is as I was on the day a young friend of mine named Ad Turner asked if I wouldn't like to spend a weekend there with him during a Christmas vacation from our university. I remember Ad's saying that it would be convenient for us to stop at Cairo, since his family lived nearby, in Mound City, an Illinois delta town, and I remember that I had only two associations with the region. Ad's town gave its name to an early jazz group, the Mound City Blue Blowers, whose records I have heard; they feature a man who took solos on comb and tissue paper. And Cairo was the birthplace of Little Egypt, the belly dancer at the first Chicago World's Fair, who seems to be a regular member of the turn-of-the-century nostalgia cast. It took a certain amount of patient explanation for Ad to clarify that what he had in mind was not some sort of wreath-laying at Little Egypt's point of humble origin, to be followed, perhaps, by an investigation of delta-region honky-tonks to discover whether there were any interesting young comb men playing progressive around there these days. My obtuseness came from my being an Easterner; to those who hunt for ducks and geese along the Mississippi flyway, "Cairo, Illinois" is one of those two-word phrases that stand for fulfillment, like "World Series" to a baseball fan, or "Kentucky Derby" to one who follows horses. There are several reasons why this is so, and the first lies in the nature of the Canada goose. It is, to begin with, a giant bird; a Canada may weigh twelve pounds or more, and its wingspread can be almost as wide as the span of a grown man's arms. A large wild duck, by contrast—say, a canvasback—might weigh three pounds and its wings extend no more than three feet. But size is only a part of it; Canada geese are, of all our waterfowl, the wariest. Slow taking off, they choose during migration the most isolated of ponds or river areas in which to rest—places surrounded by as little cover as possible through which an enemy might approach. And once settled, they post sentinels, geese that stay awake at night while the flock rests. The hearing of Canada geese is keen, their sight extraordinary, and their capacity for suspicion endless, so they are rarely fooled by decoys unless the hunter using them is completely concealed. One prepares a goose blind as one might a camouflaged bunker in trench warfare, even erasing such evidence as footprints in the mud and spent shotgun shells. The ordinary duckblind, rising as it does above the ground, will not do at all. But the geese pass through most areas so quickly on their southbound autumn journey, and the number of likely resting places is so limited, that preparation for the birds is an effort disproportionate to the chance of shooting one.

Yet one sees them; it is a characteristic of the unattainable that one must glimpse it now and then. Once, hoping to jump a duck out of hiding in the reeds in a marshy area on a bank of the Cedar river, in the next Iowa county east of ours, I heard a splashing out in the channel. I looked in time to see a pair of Canadas taking off in the dusk. They were eighty yards away, out of range for the gun I carried and the light load I was using, but in my frustration I fired in that direction anyway, and felt quite silly and ashamed. Another time, in the early morning, a goose and I met face to face. It was by the Iowa river this time, and was even sillier. I had come back to a particular long, willow-covered sandbar, having seen goose droppings on it the day before. I came out of the willows as the goose walked out of the water onto the bar, and we were no more than thirty yards apart. It took each of us a moment to recover; then I threw my cap at the goose, wanting it to fly, but it was quite deliberate, merely turning and walking away from me back into the water. It swam a fair distance as I ran to the river's edge, clumsy in hip boots, waving at it. Finally, the goose began to stroke its wings; it rose, gaining power and speed as I urged it up, and by then, though it was still in easy range, I was too excited and I missed it twice, checking my gun each time to try to hold steady on the bird. This is a child's kind of error, for the first lesson in shooting a shotgun is (of course) that to hit a bird in flight you must keep the barrel in motion, just as if you were trying to overtake and wet it with a hose. The string of shot leaves the muzzle so slowly that each time I checked my swing, I shot a yard or two behind the goose.

Generally, before Cairo, when I saw geese, they were distant and in flight. The geese come through Iowa in mild weather, and on almost any morning in the early part of the waterfowl season I am by myself in an improvised duckblind. Though it may have seemed promisingly cold and cloudy when I arrived and picked my place in the dark, the sun is too bright when it comes up, and when I see the sky grow all too clearly blue, I begin to know that the pair of wood ducks that flew over just before dawn are the only ducks I shall see in such weather. Just then, crouching, remembering that I am not here to watch the little grebe swim safely about on the water of the pothole in front of me (safe from me, at least), I conscientiously take my eyes off him. I sweep them across the horizon and see black specks out there, coming toward me. Early mallards? It is only a moment before the flight establishes itself as one of the larger and more disciplined birds. I tease myself by deciding they are cormorants—well, then, if not cormorants, blue geese or snows. But they are clearly flying in a V; they do not waver, and now I hear faintly the incredibly continuous honking of the Canada in flight. I try to answer on my duck call and I glance at the two or three goose decoys I have set out, over at one side. Then the flight goes by, hundreds of yards out of range, and it is hard to believe, though really I know better than to question it, that the geese were in any way aware of me.

But in Cairo, Ad Turner insisted, there are geese by the hundreds of thousands in plain view—virtually the whole mid-continental population, spending the winter there and highly susceptible to death by shooting. Near Cairo there is a large, Y-shaped body of water called Horseshoe lake. It is not a lake, really, but an oxbow of the Mississippi—a former channel, that is, silted away from the main body of water. And what a body of water the Mississippi is at Cairo! It is carrying with it, at that point, the water from the Missouri and the Illinois, and at the delta it is joined by the combined floods of the Ohio and the Wabash systems. All this great confluence of water from east and west seems to pause at the delta, in a pool two miles across, as if gathering itself for its concerted rush south, between Tennessee and Arkansas, Mississippi and Louisiana, to the Gulf. In the view of a migrating goose, it would seem, Horseshoe lake has always stood at the head of the South; Colonial naturalists observed geese at the lake, and before them it was a hunting ground for which Indian wars were fought. The birds began arriving in late September, were there in numbers by late October, and stayed as long as there was feed in the fields before moving on to the deeper South. Today they do not move on, for the feed never runs out at Horseshoe lake; it is now a state game preserve, administered by the Illinois Department of Conservation. "Here," reads a Cairo Chamber of Commerce folder, "[the birds are] given food and protection." And here the geese stay, along with countless ducks, all winter long. The migration has been stopped short.

Here are the birds, and within the limits of the refuge there is only one thing lacking for their winter comfort; like all waterfowl, geese must load their gizzards every day or so with sand or fine gravel to grind their food, and there is no supply of these grits at Horseshoe lake. They must be got on sandbars, or on the pebble beaches of small islands, over in the river. To reach the river, the geese must fly from the lake across a narrow strip of land, two miles wide in some places and as much as seven in others, which runs between the lake shore and the roughly parallel bend of the present channel. Dug in the strip, at intervals of two hundred yards, set by state law and as regular as stars in a flag, are hundreds of shooting pits. A low-flying bird, on his obligatory journey, is never out of range of one pit or another.

The money value of land within the strip is comparable to that of producing gold acreage. As I understand it, most of the land is leased by pit operators from farmers, who discovered one day thirty years ago that the State of Illinois had given them fortunes. The standard rate in a two-man pit is ten or fifteen dollars a man, depending on location, and there are days, when the geese are flying low and decoying well, when the first party in a given pit gets its limit (two geese per man, most years) quite early in the day, and is hustled out to make room for men who are standing by, who did not have reservations. On such days, six or even eight fees may be collected. Almost always there are men waiting, for reservations are hard come by at any price. How long the shooting season goes on each year depends on federal regulations, based on summer counts in the breeding areas; the season, which starts at the end of October ordinarily, may last anywhere from thirty to fifty days, and a short season is viewed locally as an economic disaster. I learned all this from Ad as we drove down—he was explaining that our time in the pits would cost us nothing personally, for we would be guests. "You can't get into the pits nearest the lake any other way," he said. "Not even if you'd sent for a reservation last summer. Business firms take them by the season, especially the oil companies." Our particular host was to be a man I named H. Frank Ferrell, a spectacularly successful broker and investor in commodities, chiefly cotton and rice. Ad's father had helped him get started, just after the war, and Mr. Ferrell now maintained offices in both St. Louis and Chicago, though in the fall he worked almost exclusively from a motel unit in Cairo. "That way, when he's got someone coming in to go goose hunting, Frank can rest up a few days first," Ad said. He then went on to tell me (it was a long drive down) about a cousin of his who had inherited a farm whose lands included a tiny Mississippi river island just about opposite Horseshoe lake,

[72]

GAMEBIRD

on the Missouri side of the river. On the island, the cousin has permitted a private group, which couldn't get seasonal control of facilities within the strip, to dig five goose pits. Though shooting on this island is very spotty and decidedly inferior to that along the lake, the group willingly pays—and of this Ad felt certain—an annual rental of twenty-five thousand dollars for its pits.

The pleasure of shooting geese, in itself, is not enough to explain so high a valuation on the part of the Midwest business community. There is a final pair of factors, as much a cause as an effect, and that is the lure of lust and money. "Every gambler and B-girl in Chicago can tell you the day the goose season opens down here," Ad told me. We were coming into town at last, and since long drives to hunting places generally end in an area of some degree of wilderness, I was astonished to find that we were passing roadhouses—

country night clubs with city names, including a Stork Club and a Latin Quarter. They occupied well-finished one-story buildings, for the most part, with brightly lit signs out front billing what have come to be called exotic dancers. "The people who work these places read the outdoor columns in Chicago, so they can follow the movement of the flights out of Canada," he said. "Bird watchers. They get here every year to set up for the hunters just about a week before the geese do."

It was in one of these roadhouses, its decorator-rustic bar quite deserted in the early evening, that I met our host, Frank Ferrell, who had known Ad for years. Ad and I were looking forward to a restful supper and an early sleep at Ad's house—we'd been driving all day and were to be up again by three in the morning. Mr. Ferrell started talking at once about some businessmen he was meeting shortly in town; he was perhaps not so unabashed a pirate as he seemed in talking about the situation to me, a stranger. And perhaps it was partly a matter of wanting to shock "the Professor," for he took pleasure in using the title (to which I had no claim) when he spoke to me.

"Now, I know you can see the psychology here if you just stop and think a minute, Professor," he said. He was a florid, ingratiating man in his late forties, short, muscular, and curly-haired—almost a regional appearance. Give Ad a few years and a few pounds, take away his glasses and restore the Southern accent, which he'd almost lost, and he'd be not unlike Frank Ferrell. Ad was even smiling a similar ambiguous smile as Mr. Ferrell went on. "Now, you want to get your customer or your client out on a wingding. He's probably got a wife. It ain't one in a hundred's worth doing business with don't have him a damn wife." He returned Ad's smile, having offered me this bait of bad grammar; I couldn't help smiling, too. "Well, it won't work a bit any more for him to say, 'Now, honey, I've got this important business meeting.' Hell, your wife knows all there is to know about business meetings. But listen here, how does this sound?" He adopted a tone of quiet virility, rather like that of a Western marshal on television: "'Say, honey. Some men I deal with need for me to go goose hunting with them for three, four days. There's a big flight in, down near this backwoods town in Illinois.' Now, probably this fellow, last time he had a gun in his hands, it was his Christmas BB gun and he was aiming right below the elastic on the pants of the little girl next door. Probably missed and hit himself in the foot, too, but he says, 'Haven't had too much time for hunting these past few years.' What does his wife say, Professor?''

I shook my head, recognizing this as Ad's cue, not mine, and of course Ad knew the answer. " 'Oh, darling. Do arrange to go. You love the outdoors so. It's a shame the way you're tied to your desk.' ''

"Yessir," said Mr. Ferrell. ' 'Next thing you know, she's subscribed to all the hunting and fishing magazines for him. He comes home with fifty dollars' worth of flannel shirts and a brand-new tan hunting jacket. Boots? He's gotta have at least three pairs. She changes the pictures on the wall to sporting prints—''

"Sure, Frank," Ad said. "You send them to her.''

"Well, she's the one needs convincing," Mr. Ferrell said. "But not much, usually. She likes to think of him that way. And he—well, he just always could see himself honky-tonking all night and busting geese all day." He chuckled his pirate's chuckle. "Wait till you see some of those goose hunters in the morning," he told me.

I cannot, of course, scorn such men as he was speaking of for fantasizing. Chumps they may be for making deals in the midst of excess and emotional confusion with the likes of Frank Ferrell, rested and waiting for them. But fantasizing one's role is something I have already discussed as part of hunting —part even of what I call hunting-as-I-wish-to.

It often progresses for me something like this: One begins by locating an area, judging the terrain, the vegetation, both as feed and as protection, the access to water, and whatever else the habits and preferences of a given bird require (fantasy of myself as naturalist and explorer). One must go into it, quiet and alert, carrying a loaded gun, with or without the dog (fantasy of myself as scout or Indian). One must apply certain knowledge and skills, even a primitive reason-

[75]

ing, to achieve effective surprise, or, to attract the game by calling and concealment, place oneself to advantage with regard to wind and sun. (The world is bombed out. My family and I remain. With this gun, these skills, this ammunition I have cached, I will provide for them until the crop I have planted grows.)

If the fantasies of men like Mr. Ferrell's guests run more to images of boisterous male companionship and high-production killing than of solitude, silence, and creatures that are truly wild, I am willing to acknowledge that the difference is only temperamental. I may reject their aspirations, being more deeply involved with the hunting than the shooting—but then I am not a consistently good shot—yet I am obviously in no position to be disrespectful if they, too, make of field sports a romance.

Sport at Cairo seems to me more a degradation than a fulfillment of the businessmen's kind of fantasy, and bears, of course, no resemblance to my kind whatsoever. Let me suggest the breakfast we ate with Mr. Ferrell and his guests next morning as an illustration. Breakfast to me, mornings when I hunt, is an insubstantial meal consisting largely of very hot coffee drunk in a state of lightheaded impatience to be gone, in a dark house, in a dark town; all others are asleep as I move about my kitchen in stocking feet—my boots are on the porch—barely remembering to eat the piece of toast in my hand as I try to hold off my anticipation of being outdoors by checking the equipment I piled up and checked the night before. Breakfast in Cairo is altogether different; it is intended to be hearty, leisurely, and convivial, a trencherman's bellyful of the wonderful old country-morning foods of the South— good fellows together, tucking vigorously into grits, hot breads, buttermilk cakes, country ham and sausage, home-cured bacon, and big fresh eggs, with extra-strong coffee and perhaps a tot of bourbon to settle the whole thing down. The road around Cairo and the lake has numbers of small restaurants that offer to provide this; "Hunters' Breakfast, $2.75," they advertise.

The good fellows who drove out in Frank Ferrell's Cadillac at three-thirty on the morning I am speaking of were not a likely cast of celebrants for the ritual. There was myself, already dyspeptic with foreknowledge that nothing could happen in the pits today that would reconcile this expedition with my austere mystique of hunting. (Ad's father had said the evening before, "Men ask me out to Horseshoe lake, but I never go. I guess you ought to see it once, though.") There was Mr. Ferrell—as long as he called me Professor, I was going to "Mister" him. He had three business colleagues with him, two of whom he was courting; the third he treated with good-natured contempt. There was Ad, the student, his spirits somewhat dulled with tiredness from the long drive and early rising; he seemed quite silent, and I think it was because he felt himself caught between men who would hold his high academic talents in little respect and another, myself, to whom their respect meant little. The colleague towards whom Mr. Ferrell was so derisive was named Mr. James; he was quite drunk, which made him alternately boisterous and surly. I have no recollections of the names and faces of the other two, but, like Mr. James, they were around fifty, they were out of condition, and they hadn't slept. They seemed in the curious state of being incipiently hungover, but determined to stay with it, as if the killing of geese was to be the climax of a late party, rather than an activity that deserved a day of its own.

Each packaged in his own schemes, complaints, or apprehensions, we good fellows straggled separately from the car, across gravel and around puddles, toward the door of a pretty ordinary-looking lunch counter, which was about a mile from the lake. Just at the door of the place, the Professor, the last man in, heard, out in the starry darkness to the south, a single goose calling; paused, thrilled. Churlishly, he did not mention it when he reached the table where the others sat.

And now that we have examined the fellowship, what foods were served? They had the appearance and quantity of the sort of fine country breakfast I have invoked above. But what the platters actually held was processed ham from the supermarket, sliced thin and frizzled in a skillet; bland brown-and-serve sausages, of the same quality; toasted commercial white bread; biscuits from a cardboard tube; pancakes with that funny sour aftertaste of the ready-mixed; and a cheap standard-brand syrup in its original bottle. The coffee was as bad as lunch-counter coffee, contrary to popular opinion, usually is, and nobody ate the eggs. (No evaluation can be given of the tot of bourbon, which was drunk from the bottle, for the Professor, prig to the end, declined, saying, when pressed, that he didn't think it went well with syrup.)

It was a quarter to four. There were a dozen other goose hunters in the place. There were funny hunting and fishing signs on the wall.

At four-thirty, we were still there. We had discussed the ease with which the football team representing Ad's and my university had beaten Notre Dame a few weeks before. We had discussed the hostess in a certain Cairo night club, and heard Frank Ferrell tell Mr. James, with coarse irony, that he, James, had better get a cab and go on back there if he thought so much of her. I had been up and away from the table twice to stand outside the door, listening for calling geese. Each time, there were a few more voices, but still faint and far away, and the sky was beginning to lighten. On my way back in the second time, seeing that yet more coffee was being poured at our table, I stopped at the counter and bought a goose call, an object that resembles a fat, flared wooden whistle.

Mr. James, hoping, I suppose, to turn some of the weight of group irony away from himself, said, "Aw, Professor, you pay five bucks for that thing?"

I nodded.

"I'd have sold you one just like it for three," he said. "That's what they cost in town."

"Boy, Jamesie, you're a big dealer," said Frank Ferrell.

Mr. James had been to Cairo once before. He had made a deer-hunting trip to Michigan once, too, he had told us, with a bunch of men he knew. He had an almost new deer-hunting cap, which he wore through breakfast, to prove it; it was bright red, and about as appropriate to hunting waterfowl as a scarecrow might be out among the decoys.

Ad and I left them at breakfast, after a while, to stand in the parking lot listening to the geese. The chorus of honking was getting fuller all the time. I remarked that it was going to be a clear day, and Ad said that was too bad, because cloudy skies kept the birds lower. I asked if he had hunted here often, and Ad said no, he had gone to the public shooting ground now and then as a kid, but, because his father disliked them, he had never been to the commercial pits before.

Then Mr. Ferrell came out with the others, crying, "Come on! Let's kill geese," and as we started away in the car, he explained how he'd decided to deploy us. He had three pits and had engaged three professional callers. The two men whose business he was courting would be with one; Ad and I would share another. He'd keep Mr. James with him and watch how a real goose hunter hit 'em, said Frank Ferrell, who never seemed to let up. I'd begun to feel a good bit of sympathy for Mr. James.

While the middle-aged men bickered (the businessmen aloud, the Professor in invisible grimaces in the dark interior of the Cadillac), the car moved on, along a macadam road, and a vision began to take shape on the immediate right—a sheet of pale-grey water, stretching out of sight in the pre-dawn from the cypress trees at the edge of the road. I opened the car window on that side, and all at once the chorus of honking was like a thousand oboes warming up with comic notes. The reefs of black rock in the grey water, some within fifty yards of the road, were separating into creatures that were shifting, stretching their wings.

"Those can't be geese," I muttered.

"They're safe in there," Ad said. "It's the refuge."

"But crowded in like this, with cars going by?"

"They're fed in there," Ad said, and it seemed too silly even for a disgruntled professor to reply, in the character of a goose, that he'd rather starve. Anyway, I was an excited professor, too; nothing in the circumstances or the company could completely spoil the exhilaration of seeing so many Canada geese so close.

We turned left, onto a gravel drive, drove a hundred yards away from the lake, and stopped at the edge of a turnaround. A trailer was parked nearby, and there was a shack beside it, brightly lighted, which we entered. The shack was full of men like ourselves, talking rather quietly on the whole; there was an occasional burst of boisterousness, but most of the goose hunters seemed tired or strained. I judged that most of them were sober, and I felt a certain relief at this.

There was a counter in the shack, at which the proprietor's wife sold coffee, snacks, and shotgun shells. She also kept Frank Ferrell's guns for him, since he came out there so often and didn't like to carry them back and forth. I have to smile when I remember the shotgun situation. I was shooting two that season, and had hesitated for some time over which to bring along. One was a long-barrelled Browning automatic 12-gauge, which I generally used in duck hunting, the other a lovely old double-barrelled Parker, of the same gauge. The Parker was really too light for anything but the short-range loads used in quail shooting, but it broke down in such a way as to pack more neatly than the big gun. I'd decided it wouldn't hurt to shoot goose loads in the Parker for the single day I'd be there, and the rest of my hesitation had been over whether it wouldn't seem snobbish for me to show up with such an elegant little weapon. What makes me smile now is that the elegance of the Parker didn't register at all; my host, though he undoubtedly knew shotguns well enough to recognize its quality, felt about the Parker as I did about Mr. James' red hat. It simply didn't fit the occasion, and Mr. Ferrell's tone was commiserative when he told me that he didn't have more than four of the weapons that were stored there at the shack—Browning automatics, like the one I'd left behind, but specially chambered to shoot three-inch magnum shells instead of the regular two-and-three-quarter-inch kind. "Cairo specials," Mr. Ferrell said, showing me the Brownings. "These'll reach up and get 'em." And, indeed, nearly everyone I saw that morning was equipped with one, including the professional callers, who arrived just a minute or two after we did.

The caller who guided Ad and me through the dark to Pit No. 7 was named Dave. He didn't have much to say as we left the shack, except to ask us to check our guns to be sure they were unloaded. Then we started off through the dark and muddy field, walking parallel to the highway, which was about a hundred yards to our right. All around, little groups of men were sloshing off toward their stations, and the walking was so difficult that one heard little conversation.

I think the biggest shock of the whole trip for me may have been a feature of the location of Pit 7. It was in the second row, and since the rows were offset, there was no other pit in line between it and the highway and the lake. But if there was no other pit right in front of us, there was something else, directly in line with the lake, which I still find hard to believe: there was a tavern. It stood at the edge of the highway, its neon sign burning steadily dead ahead. It seemed impossible to me that geese wouldn't flare away from it in all directions. The wind was towards us, off the lake, and it carried the sound of the jukebox to us faintly whenever a customer going in or out opened the door.

"The geese don't pay no attention to it," said Dave, the caller, when I asked about the tavern.

"Maybe they like the music," Ad suggested. "Like cows in a well-run dairy barn."

There was a grunt of doubtful amusement which came from neither Ad nor Dave, and I saw that a fourth man was with us, standing only a step away in the darkness. It was Mr. James.

"Follow the wrong guide?" Dave asked, and it did seem an easy enough error for anyone to have made as the various groups crisscrossed the unfamiliar ground.

Whether it was error or not, Mr. James wanted to stay with us. On his previous trip to Cairo, he said, sharing a pit with Frank Ferrell had meant letting the host shoot the two geese of Mr. James' limit, as well as his own. And although the law permits no more than two men and a guide per pit, Dave said it didn't matter to him if Mr. James stayed, and neither Ad nor I had any objection. The pit into which we all scrambled was actually more of a trench, perhaps eight feet long, five wide, and seven deep. The front half, nearer the lake, was sheltered at ground level by a wooden cover, angling slightly up to form a partial roof. Under the roof there was a bench, onto which Mr. James slumped at once. It was too dark to tell, but I thought his eyes were closed, which seemed sensible enough—there were still twenty minutes before sunrise, when shooting could begin. Along the rear wall was a step, on which one stood to shoot. Anyone who stayed forward and under the roof would be invisible even to a goose flying directly overhead. Since the pit was both floored and walled with boards, standing in it was essentially like being inside a large, sunken wooden box. There was a little sportsman's stove under the roof for hand-warming when necessary; otherwise the pit was unequipped and unpainted. I had heard about pits with radios and coffee-makers and cushioned resting places, but I suppose they are the fully private ones. The only lavishness here was outside. As the day grew lighter, I could see that our pit stood in a field in which corn had been grown and knocked down, leaving stalk and stubble, which material had been used to disguise the top of our box; in front of each pit were arranged something like forty goose decoys, of a kind made by a firm called Herter's. I have Herter's catalogue, which lists these decoys at forty-eight dollars a dozen in large-quantity orders.

Ad and I spent the twenty minutes before sunrise standing on the rear step, looking past the decoys and the tavern, towards the lake, while Dave sat with Mr. James on the bench beneath us, stolidly facing our knees. They were the best twenty minutes of the day. When we started our watch, most of the geese and most of the ducks who shared the lake with them were still rafted up, as they had been while sleeping, but now and again a single bird would rise a few feet off the water, try his wings, and drop into a different position, and it wasn't long before this expression of energy began to communicate itself to others. Now small groups of birds, four or five at a time, would rise together and fly laterally along the lake shore, and soon these little groups began to make the turn and to come stroking out across the fields in which we were hidden.

I was watching out to the left of the tavern, Ad to the right; six or eight minutes might have gone by when I felt him poke my shoulder. I turned my head and saw a pair of geese flying towards us across the road. They came over the front-row pits, their wing strokes smooth and slow, gaining altitude slightly, black in the half-light. We both crouched, lowering our eyes to the level of the roof edge in front of us, peering up from under our hatbrims, and to me, a duck hunter with the long autumn behind me, during which a mallard in flight had come to seem enormous, the size of these geese was awesome. They went directly over our heads, and it seemed to me that they moved so slowly in the air and were so close that it would be almost impossible to miss such a shot.

"What about the range of those?" I whispered to Ad as they sailed over us.

"Pretty extreme," Ad whispered back. Then he added, in a normal voice, "I remember my father telling me when I was a kid, if a goose looks duck-size, don't shoot; if it looks goose-size, it's still a little out of range; when it suddenly swells and looks cow-size, then you've got a chance."

The next group that came over was even higher, but it was more exciting, for there were twenty geese, and the light had improved enough so that I could see their colors. I watched them start from far out on the lake, shifting around, some rising and circling, calling, waiting for others to join them, and finally forming up and starting for us, at which point their honking ceased. This group actually came directly over the tavern roof (to the strains of what I think was "Rock Around the Clock"), and I judged that they cleared it by at least five times its height. If the building was thirty feet, or ten yards, high, as I estimated it, then the geese must have been sixty yards up; in addition, the line they flew was something like twenty yards to the left of the pit, making the total range eighty yards or more, but they seemed at least goose-size to me—maybe bigger.

"You mean that's not a shot?" I asked Ad.

"Maybe for an expert, shooting three-inch magnums," Ad said.

"But I can see the white patches on their cheeks."

"How far away could you see a white cigarette package on a dark background?" Ad asked. "That's the size of those patches."

The air above the lake was full of waterfowl now, though I don't suppose the birds in flight amounted to five per cent of those staying on the water. The sun was very close to being up, behind us in the east, so that the highest birds gleamed now as they flew. A big flight of these gleaming geese—perhaps a hundred of them—formed into a V over the lake, and as they came over the highway I was speculating on whether so large and formal a formation might not indicate some longer journey than merely to the river, when I heard the first shot of the morning, from the pit in front of us to the right. Sunrise for hunters is not a condition of the sky but rather a particular minute on one's watch, and I hadn't been checking mine; I was both surprised that shooting time had come and confused at not being able to locate which geese were being shot at. "Where are they?" I yelled at Ad, as eight or ten more shotguns exploded, first in the front row, now in the pits on either side of us.

"Those," Ad said, pointing to the high hundred, which had broken formation and were scrambled all over the sky, most of them wheeling back towards the lake.

"They're a quarter of a mile up," I objected.

"Something like that." It was a new voice, that of Dave the caller, who, with Mr. James, now pushed up onto the step with us.

"Didn't they drop any?" Mr. James asked. I think the firing had waked him up.

"I don't think the shot would even carry that high," Ad said. "Much less kill anything."

There was a pause, while we watched the sky clear of geese. Then Dave said, "Suppose someone was shooting buckshot, and he did hit; the goose'd be two miles away by the time he came down. Look over left." We looked. "There's some low enough."

Over the adjacent field, six or seven hundred yards from us, a line of ten geese was crossing at treetop height. As we looked, one staggered in midair, folded, and dropped straight down.

"Someone's starting the day right," said Dave, as we watched a second goose fall, recover, and flapping its good wing wildly, turn back to the lake. About the time the sound of the gunfire from the opening volley reached us—it sounded like fifty shots—we saw the cripple hit again, but it kept flying, and Mr. James said, "He'll make the lake, then die there. We had two like that last time I was here."

[84]

"Won't someone go in and pick him up?" I asked, and they all, more or less together, informed me that it wasn't allowed. Dave said he'd bet three quarters of the geese hit here died in the lake. That would be a frightening estimate, since the annual kill of birds at Horseshoe lake, as announced in the Cairo Chamber of Commerce folder, is over twenty-five thousand, out of a goose population of two hundred thousand. Dave also said that many geese took so little lead that you couldn't even tell they were hit at the time, but the pellets would work into a body organ after a while and poison them. Ad seemed to doubt this, and some weeks later I asked a game biologist about Dave's account of the poisoning. The biologist thought it probably happened occasionally, but added that most of the waterfowl that die annually from lead poisoning do so because they actually swallow pellets with their sand or food. I cannot find any figures on how many victims may be claimed each year, but all authorities seem to agree that it is a serious problem. Swallowing six pellets of No. 6 shot, it has been found, is enough to kill a mallard, a bird one quarter the size of a Canada goose. If I am right in assigning each gunner in the thirty-pit area in which we were shooting a daily average expenditure of a box of twenty-five No. 4 high-brass shells, each shell containing some two hundred shot pellets, there must be an accumulation of around half a million pellets per day on that small acreage.

We had been watching the survivors of the little flock that had been shot into in the next field making their escapes, and we saw two of them head over our own field, gaining speed and altitude all the time and greeted by constant harmless gunfire from each new pit over which they flew. Then things were quiet for a few minutes, and it was Mr. James who said, "Here come three."

They were just leaving the water, out in front of us, undecided so far what line of flight to take, and Dave motioned us down and began to call. He used no mechanical goose call such as the one I had in my pocket; he did it by voice, and it was uncannily accurate—a rising, two-noted honk in loud falsetto. Peering out at ground level, I could see the geese responding, noticing our decoys.

"They might come in," Dave said, down almost as low as we were. He resumed calling, omitting the lower note. Other men, just as good as Dave, were calling in the other pits now, but he seemed to have the birds' attention, for he was raising his gun. Ad, Mr. James, and I raised ours, too, but the tension only lasted an instant. There was a gun blast from nearby, and all four of us stood up and watched our geese flare and return to the lake untouched. Someone in the front-row pit to the right had tried a wild shot, at over a hundred yards, as the geese came towards our decoys.

Mr. James was indignant, as I was inclined to be, too. Dave shrugged it off. "You can't hardly ever work them right any more," he said. He glanced at his wristwatch, and I thought I knew what was on his mind—that it was going to be a long day's work getting limits for these first patrons today, and not much chance of picking up late clients for extra pay.

Those three were the closest thing we had to a shot in the first two hours of the day. The geese were not moving off the lake in any great numbers, and such few as did seemed to fall into the same pattern as ours had. They were shot at high or far off, forced higher or farther off. They were hit occasionally, though it was after seven o'clock before a bird was brought down in the field in which we were shooting. This particular goose came in from behind, and wasn't seen immediately. Dave pointed the bird out as it was lowering towards some decoys by one of the pits four rows behind us.

"They don't see him yet," Dave said to Ad and me. Mr. James was below, sleeping again. A moment later there was a nine-shot fusillade; guns are plugged at three shots each, and there were two men and a caller out there. The goose was hit, quite well hit, and it went gliding off on broken wings, with no chance this time of making the lake.

"The caller must have shot," I said, surprised.

"We generally do," said Dave. "Get ready, now." The injured goose was still gliding, gliding towards our pit, in fact.

"Should we shoot?"

The pit immediately behind and to the left opened fire as the bird flapped by them and came into range for us. Apparently we were expected to shoot, to help finish the goose off, so

[86]

Ad and I dutifully leveled on it, and I was aware of Mr. James struggling up beside me. The bird was no more than twenty feet off the ground and was virtually dead in the air when Ad's magnum and my lighter load hit and dropped it. Even Mr. James got off a shot, though I don't think his gun had reached his shoulder when he fired. In any case, the bird fell straight, lay absolutely still.

"You got him without me," Dave said, as if continuing our conversation about callers shooting. I didn't see what difference it made, but I suppose flattery is part of any trade that involves tips in addition to payment. Anyway, nothing anyone could say was going to persuade me that what we'd just done resembled wing shooting.

Mr. James was pushing at me in some excitement, since my corner of the pit was closest to where the goose had fallen, urging me to climb out and pick it up.

I didn't want to be offensive, so I put as a question what I felt like saying flatly. "But it's not ours, is it? What about the guys in the back row who shot it?"

"It's the rule here, Professor," Dave said, rather severely. (I don't know where in hell *he* picked the title up.) "Any bird you hit while it's still in the air is yours, if you're the last to hit it." Then, perhaps feeling that some explanation would be reasonable: "These high geese they shoot, they might land anywhere. You'd have men jumping out of pits all over the field to claim geese, some of them drunk, mad, loaded guns . . ."

There was no arguing with that. I climbed out, leaving my gun behind, to get the smashed carcass out of the mud; I have already mentioned how I felt toward it. What I have not said is that Mr. James, and the sympathy I felt for him, were on my mind. I knew that on his previous trip to Cairo he'd gone home gooseless, and I was thinking of another of the good moments in the kind of hunting I enjoy—the return home with game. Once, early in my waterfowling days, I came into our kitchen, after hours on the river, to where my wife was ironing.

"All right, Nimrod," said my wife, not looking up, accustomed to my coming back empty-handed that season. "Just

[87]

put all the ducks on the table.''

But I had a pintail and a mallard. It was the first time I'd ever come home with more than one duck, and it had been more than a week since I'd even had a single. "Kitchen table?" I asked, trying to say it mildly. When I picked up that goose at Cairo, I was remembering her pleasure for me, and our two excited children carrying the birds around as if they were stuffed toys. I wished such a moment for Mr. James, and so, when I got back to the pit with the goose, I gave it to him.

Mr. James was very pleased. He grinned, and grasped the goose by the neck, just under the head, and hung it over his shoulder, and a kind of energy came into his manner. "Excuse me, boys," he said. "Which pit's old Frank Ferrell in now?"

Dave told him, and he climbed briskly out, and something suggested to me that the psychological balance of whatever business dealing was going on might take a new turn now, because Mr. Ferrell, the host and expert, hadn't produced the first kill for the men he was entertaining. Mr. James was going to have a moment, even though it wasn't precisely the one I'd had in mind.

Neither Ad nor I fired a shot again until nearly ten that morning. The geese, as Dave kept saying fretfully, were not moving at all well. An occasional stray or small group would cross, and from time to time one was taken in pretty much the manner of the one that had fallen to us. I remember only two clean kills in our particular field; both were dropped with long pass shots, which Dave said must have hit in the head. But most of the thousands of geese we'd seen on the water at dawn were still sitting there at ten; the men waiting at the headquarters shack for pit room had driven away long since, and Dave remarked that his last hope for a generally good day—that a federal plane might fly over to count the geese, thus stirring them up—was about gone. There was a good deal of climbing in and out of pits—visiting back and forth, I suppose, or men returning to the parking lot for coffee or a drink.

For the past twenty minutes, I had been trying out my goose call, attempting to imitate Dave's flawless vocal reproduction, with mostly comic results. Dave had just finished saying that he never had even tried a mechanical call, that he'd learned to do it by voice as a boy and that he had been working in the pits, off and on, since he was fourteen, when Ad said, "Want a duck?"

I looked toward the lake and saw a stray mallard that was virtually diving at us—the kind of bird I'd hunted with such intensity and devotion all fall. I remember shaking my head, thinking it looked ridiculously small, mosquito-size, and just then I saw, over the tavern, two geese in flight. I touched Dave, he looked and touched Ad, and we all three crouched.

"I won't call," Dave whispered. "Nobody else sees them."

I made myself stay down until the geese came into sight, directly over our opening. They were pretty high, looking goose-size, not cow-size, but unalarmed, and their movement seemed so slow and deliberate that I believed I could hit one. The leading one was on Ad's side, and I let it go by, raised my gun, pointed carefully at the other, followed steadily, increased the speed of my swing until the gun barrel pointed out well ahead of it, for I remembered about lead shots, and fired confidently. Ad shot almost simultaneously. Both geese flared, unscathed, and headed for upper air, their wing strokes doubling in speed.

I was furious at myself. "Damn it," I said. "I must have checked."

"No, you were swinging," Dave said. "You were way behind, though. That was about an eighty-yard shot, at maybe sixty miles an hour."

I never really solved the lead problem. I had perhaps half a dozen more shots, for we stayed grimly on until the pits closed at three that afternoon. We released Dave at lunchtime. We became as bad as anyone else in the pits that day, trying the stupid long shots, trying anything. There was one goose I did hit. He came in behind us, and I turned and shot without thinking it out, and shot well. I shot again as he started to come down. Ad did, too. One or the other of us hit him in the head, and he dropped close to us, our one legitimate bird.

In the last hour, when the geese were returning from the

river, they seemed to come over our field quite frequently, and quite low, dropping past us towards refuge on the lake. I had, by then, learned to produce something like a honk on my goose call, and there were a couple of groups, it seemed to me, that were working for me, though neither was permitted to reach our pit. The first was scattered by shooting, and what happened to the second seems to me almost just retribution for the way I had fallen into the style of Cairo hunting in the deterioration of the long day. The group, six or seven, was flying towards us and dropping lower, when a man simply climbed out of one of the pits behind us. He didn't see the geese coming, and didn't think to look; he climbed out, wearing a red hunting cap like Mr. James', and ambled off toward the headquarters shack. The geese flared away, of course, to the accompaniment of the inevitable cannonade of futile shots. The man in the red hat stopped and looked up in surprise, and was apparently chagrined. It would have been Ad's and my best chance of the day.

At three, we went in, Ad carrying our single goose, for it seemed to me that his family's hospitality deserved some return. When we got back to the parking area, there were more dead geese around than I'd expected; several pits in the last row had got pit limits, and a number of individuals, of whom Frank Ferrell was one, had done well. Mr. Ferrell's party was looking pretty dazed by now, but on the whole contented. While the others of our group were getting their geese tagged by the man who operated the pits, I strolled over to look at a particularly fine bird that a hunter was holding up, with its wings spread, while a partner took his photograph. When the picture-taking was finished, the man caught my eye and smiled; it was one of those small situations in which one must say something casual, and my remark couldn't have been more so: "They're really enormous, aren't they?"

"Want him?" the man replied. "I don't know what to do with it."

"Eat it," I said. "They're supposed to be wonderful."

"You eat it," the man said, and pressed the goose on me. Then I saw that the caller who'd worked with Mr. Ferrell was giving a goose to Ad ("His kids won't eat them," Ad explained afterward). In fact, a great many geese were being passed around. Hardly anybody seemed to want them. I think a few were even left behind, since each of us could carry off no more than the daily limit of two.

As for Mr. James, his point had been made, I suppose, when he arrived at the Ferrell pit that morning with the first bird of the day. Now he insisted that I must have that same battered carcass back again, after all. When I accepted it, it seemed to me less a Canada goose than a new bird in modern ornithology, a Cairo albatross.

I have a bird book, dated 1868, that describes Canada geese and gives their wintering grounds as Arkansas and Louisiana. I don't know about Arkansas, but a year or two ago I talked to a Louisiana hunter, a man in his sixties, who told me of hunting Canada geese in his state as a young man. Since Illinois has begun to feed the geese at Horseshoe lake,

YES, WE EAT GAME

this man said, there have been none to hunt in Louisiana. He was fairly bitter about it. "They intercept them all," he said. "It's a whole state acting like a game hog."

Here is sour comfort for you, friends in Louisiana: no idea that is popular, financially beneficial, and brings regional celebrity will go unimitated for long in our culture. In north-central Missouri, well within the funnel-shaped outline of the Mississippi flyway and at a place that southbound autumn flights of Canada geese pass three hundred miles before they get to Cairo, there is something being developed called Swan lake. Already they are able to hold eighty to ninety thousand Canada geese at Swan lake for fall shooting. Some of the pits there are controlled by the Missouri Conservation Commission and assigned on a daily lottery basis, but there are currently at least six commercial shooting places, as well as a scattering of strictly private pits with padlocked covers on them when they're not in use. I went there not long ago, assured that it was different from Cairo, but the only real difference is that the honky-tonk has not been quite established yet. There is the same waiting line of men without reservations, the same feeling of "Hurry up and kill, please, to make room for others." There are the same lavish spreads of decoys, the same well-dug pits placed as close together as the law allows, so that this, like Cairo, is merely a shooting place. The hunting has been prearranged, like the flour in the ready-mixed pancakes. Professional callers are rarer at Swan lake than at Cairo, but the clients are the same—spoiling one another's chances with high shots, prodigal as schoolboys with their ammunition, and here and there sporting a red cap or an amber bottle. No, this is no hunting place; it is another elaborate outdoor shooting gallery, with live geese for targets. With such a central attraction operating at Swan lake, I cannot suppose that the other games and shows of a grown man's amusement park will be long in developing.

4. In Fields Near Home

ANY AUTUMN. EVERY AUTUMN, SO LONG AS MY luck holds and my health, and if I win the race. The race is a long, slow one that has been going on since I started to hunt again. The race is between my real competence at hunting, gradually developing, and, gradually fading, the force of the fantasies which have sustained me while the skills are still weak. If the fantasies fade before the competence is really mine, I am lost as a hunter because I cannot enjoy disgust. I will have to stop, after all, and look for something else.

So I shan't write of any autumn, or every autumn, but of last autumn, the most recent and the most skilled. And not of any day, but a particular day, when things went really well.

7:45 No clock need wake me.

7:55 While I am pulling on my socks, taking simple-minded satisfaction in how clean my feet are from last night's bath, relishing the feel against them of heavy, close-knit wool, fluffed and warmed and freshly washed, the phone rings downstairs. I go down to answer it, stocking-footed and springysoled, but I am not wondering particularly who the caller is. I am still thinking about clean feet and socks. Even twenty years after infantry training, I can remember what it is like to walk too far with wet lint, cold dirt, and callouses between the flesh and the matted stocking sole, and what it is like to long for the sight of one's own unfamiliar feet and for the opportunity to make them comfortable and unrepulsive.

It is Mr. Burton on the phone.

"Hello?"

"Yeah. Hi, Mr. Burton."

"Say, I've got some news. I called a farmer friend of mine, up north of Waterloo last night. He says there're lots of birds, his place hasn't been hunted for a week."

"Uh-huh."

"I thought we'd go up there instead."

Mr. Burton is a man in his late fifties whom I've known for two or three years. He took me duck hunting once, to a privately leased place, where we did quite well. I took him pheasant hunting in return, and he has a great admiration for my dog Moon. He wants his nephew to see Moon work. The kid has a day off from school today.

But: "The boy can't go after all," Mr. Burton says. "His mother won't let him. But say, I thought we might pick up Cary Johnson—you know him don't you? The attorney. He wants to go. We'll use his car."

Boy, I can see it. It's what my wife calls the drive-around. Mr. Burton will drive to my house; he will have coffee. We will drive to Johnson's house. We will have coffee while Johnson changes to different boots—it's colder than he expected. Johnson will meet a friend who doesn't want to hold us fellows up, but sure would like to go if we're sure there's room. We will have coffee at the drugstore while Johnson's friend goes home, to check with his wife and change. It will be very hot in the drugstore in hunting clothes; the friend will phone and say he can't go after all. Now nothing will be holding us up but the decision to change back to my car, because Johnson's afraid my dog's toenails will rip his seat covers. Off for Waterloo, two hours away (only an hour and a half if Mr. Burton knew exactly how to find the farm.) The farmer will have given us up and gone to town. Now that we're here, though, we will drive into town to the feed store, and . . .

"Hell, Mr. Burton," I say. ' 'I'm afraid I can't go along."

"Sure you can. We have a date, don't we?"

"I'll be glad . . ."

"Look, I know you'll like Johnson. That's real hunting up there—I'll bet you five right now we all get limits."

I will not allow myself to think up an excuse. "I'm sorry," I say. "I'll be glad to take you out around here." I even emphasize *you* a little to exclude Johnson, whoever he is.

"I pretty much promised my farmer friend . . . Oh, look now, is it a matter of having to be back or something?"

"I'm sorry."

"Well, I told him we'd come to Waterloo. There are some things I have to take up to him."

Not being among the things Mr. Burton has to take to his farmer friend, nor my dog either, I continue to decline. Hot damn. Boy, boy, boy. A day to myself.

Ten months a year I'm a social coward, but it's hard to bully me in hunting season, especially with clean socks on.

8:05 Shaving: Unnecessary. Shaving for fun, with a brand new blade.

Thinking: Mr. Burton, sir, if your hunting is good, and you

get a limit of three birds, in two hours	2
& it takes two hours driving to get there	2
& an hour of messing around on arrival	1
& an hour for lunch	1
& two hours to get back and run people home	2
	8

you will call it a good hunt, though the likelihood is, since you are no better shot than I, that other men will have shot one or more of your three birds. There is a shoot-as-shoot-can aspect to group hunts; it's assumed that all limits are combined, and it would be considered quite boorish to suggest that one would somehow like to shoot one's own birds.

Thinking: suppose I spend the same eight hours hunting, and it takes me all that time to get three pheasants. In my eccentric mind, that would be four times as good a hunt, since I would be outdoors four times as long. And be spared all that goddamn conversation.

Chortling at the face behind the lather: pleasant fellow, aren't you?

Thinking: God I like to hunt near home. The known covert, the familiar trail. And in my own way, and at my own pace, and giving no directions, nor considering any other man's. Someday I'll own the fields behind my house, and there'll be nothing but a door between me and the game—pick up a gun, call a dog, slip out. They'll know where I've gone.

Thinking as I see the naked face, with no lather to hide behind now: I'll take Mr. Burton soon. Pretty nice man. I'll find him birds, too, and stand aside while he shoots, as I did for Jake, and Grannum, and that short guy, whatever his name was, looked so good; Moon and I raised three birds for him, one after another, all in nice range, before he hit one. Damn. That's all right. I don't mind taking people. It's a privilege to go out with a wise hunter; a pleasure to go out with one of equal skill, if he's a friend; and a happy enough responsibility to take an inexperienced one sometimes. Eight or ten pheasants given away like that this season? Why not? I've got twelve already myself, more than in any season before and this one's barely ten days old. And for the first time, missed fewer than I've hit.

Eggs?

8:15 Sure! Eggs! Three of them! Fried in hot olive oil, so they puff up. With lemon juice. Tabasco. Good. Peppery country sausage, and a stack of toast. Yes, hungry. Moon comes in.

"Hey, boy. Care to go?"

Wags.

"Wouldn't you just rather stay home today and rest up?"

Wags, grins.

"Yeah, wag. If you knew what I said you'd bite me."

Wags, stretches, rubs against me.

"You'd better have some breakfast, too." I go to the refrigerator. Moon is a big dog, a Weimaraner, and he gets a pound of hamburger mornings when he's going to be working. I scoop out the cold ground meat from its paper carton, and pat it between my hands into a ball. I roll it across the floor, under his dignified nose. This is a silly game we play; he follows it with his eyes, then pounces as if it really were a ball, trapping it with a paw. My wife, coming in from the yard, catches us.

"Having a game of ball," I say.

"What is it you're always telling the children about not making the same joke twice?"

"Moon thinks it's funny."

"Moon's a very patient dog. I see you're planning to work again today."

I smile. I know this lady. "I really should write letters," I say.

"They can wait, can't they?" She smiles. She likes me to go hunting. She's still not really convinced that I enjoy it—when we were first married I liked cities—but if I do enjoy it, then certainly I must go.

Yes, letters can wait. Let them ripen a few more days. It's autumn. Maybe some of them will perish in the frost if I leave them another week or two—hell, even the oldest ones are barely a month old.

8:35 Putting shells into the loops in the pockets of my hunting jacket, I am smug, with the particular smugness of a man who has managed to serve his prejudice. Yesterday afternoon, at an unfamiliar sporting-goods store, I found some low-brass sixes. Translation and explanation (Ballistics? Nonsense. Devils don't quote scripture these days, they quote science): Low-brass shells carry less powder charge than high-brass ones. Shell-manufacturers have gone absolutely wild, manufacturing and promoting overpowered shells. Rather like car-manufacturers, with less reason. I suppose it's because they can charge more money per box. High-brass shells are loud, jarring, expensive, and they pattern with all the beauty of a handful of mud thrown against a white fence (and then, believe it or not, there are magnums which are the same thing but worse). The essence of a good shell is pattern—when you shoot one into a thirty-inch paper circle, there should be holes made by the individual pellets spread evenly all over it; the only commercial shells sold today that will do this are the cheapest, the lightly loaded kind, with a low-brass collar at the base, made for trapshooters and penny pinchers. These can be found readily enough in small-shot sizes (7½ and 8), but in the right sizes for pheasants (6 and 5) low-brass are as hard to find as a loaf of good bread.

Hunters have been sold, by unrelenting advertising, on the preposterous idea that a heavy charge will get more birds because it will give more range. My witness, heh heh.

ME: Just what proportion of men hunting today have the skill to take advantage of more than thirty yards of range?

DEVILS: Well, not many of course.

ME: Isn't the art in knowing which shots to try, rather than in firing at every bird you see no matter how far off?

DEVILS: Yes, but . . .

ME: Isn't it true that a damn-fool long-range shot may cripple a bird imperceptibly, so the shooter doesn't even know he hit?

DEVILS: Ummm . . .

ME: The typical use for a long-range shell would be in pass-shooting at waterfowl, would it not? What per cent of the shots during normal hunting days are like that? About one per cent?

DEVILS: Two! Two! At least two!

ME: So hunters are induced to carry a hundred per cent of the shells useful in two per cent of the hunting situations? What about these Big Bertha shells on the short-range shots? Isn't it true that a heavily charged shell causes misses, going out the barrel of a full-choked gun in a clump about the size of a billiard ball for the first twenty yards?

If the devils had known I was on this case, they'd never have shown up in court. I finish loading up the left pocket, my second-shot pocket. Because it's cold this morning—the sun is just now coming out—and rather windy, I put brush loads in the first-shot pocket, on the right. Translation and explanation, devils concurring this time: Brush loads spread most quickly of all. Pheasants ought to lie tight on a morning like this, letting Moon and me get right up on them before they fly.

I trot happily downstairs, Moon crowding me all the way; back to the kitchen, smile at the good pheasant weather out the window, give my good old wife a kiss, and my good old four-year-old boy a pat, and am out the door—to serve a prejudice builds confidence. Now there's a charge that does need increasing. Low-brass shells make the high-brass hunter.

8:45 I never have to tell Moon to get in the car. He's on his hind legs, with his paws on the window, before I reach it. As I get in, start the car, and warm it up, an image comes into my mind of a certain hayfield. It's nice the way this happens; no reasoning, no weighing of one place to start against another. As if the image were projected directly by the precise feel of a certain temperature, a certain wind strength—from sensation to picture without intervening thought. As we drive, I can see just how much the hay should be waving in the wind, just how the shorter grass along the highway will look, going from white to wet as the frost melts off—for suddenly the sun's quite bright.

8:55 I stop, and look at the hayfield, and if sensation projected an image of it into my mind, now it's as if my mind could project the same image, expanded, onto a landscape. The hay *is* waving, just that much. The frost *is* starting to melt.

"Whoa, Moon. Stay."

I have three more minutes to think it over. Pheasant hunting starts at nine.

"Moonie. Quiet, boy."

He is quivering, whining, throwing his weight against the door.

I think they'll be in the hay itself—tall grass, really, not a seeded crop; anyway, not in this shorter stuff that grows in the first hundred yards or so along the road. Right?

What time?

[99]

8:58 Well. Yeah. Whoa.

The season's made its turn at last. Heavy frost every morning now. No more mosquitos, flies. Cold enough so that it feels good to move, not so cold that I'll need gloves: perfect. No more grasshoppers, either. A sacrifice, in a way—pheasants that feed on hoppers, in open fields, are wilder and taste better than the ones that hang around corn.

The season's made its turn in another sense—the long progression of openings is over: Rabbits, squirrels, September 15. Geese, October 5. Ducks, snipe, October 27. Quail, November 3. Pheasant, November 10. That was ten days ago. Finally, everything that's ever legal may be hunted. The closings haven't started yet. Amplitude. Best time of the year. Whoa.

8:59 Whoa! Now it's me quivering, whining, but I needn't throw my weight against the door—open it. I step out, making Moon stay. I uncase the gun, look at it with love, throw the case in the car; load. Breathe cold air. Good. Look around. Fine.

"Come on, Moonie. Nine o'clock."

9:00 I start on the most direct line through the short grass, towards the tall, not paying much attention to Moon, who must relieve himself. I think this is as much a matter of nervous tension as it is of regularity.

"Come on, Moon," I call, keeping to my line. "This way, boy."

He thinks he's got a scent back here, in the short grass; barely enough for a pheasant to hide in, and much too thin for cold-day cover.

"Come, Moon. Hyeahp."

It must be an old scent. But he disregards me. His stub of a tail begins to go as he angles off, about thirty yards from where I am; his body lowers just a little and he's moving quickly. I am ignorant in many things about hunting, but there's one thing I know after eight years with this dog: if you bother to hunt with a dog at all, believe what he tells you. Go where he says the bird is, not where you think it ought to be.

I move that way, going pretty quickly myself, still convinced it's an old foot-trail he's following, and he stops in a half-point, his head sinking down while his nose stays up, so that the grey neck is almost in a shallow S-curve.

"He's not there any more, Moonie," I say, still advancing, cautiously, and *WHIRRR*. Clap go the wings. *CUKCUK-CUK-CUK-CUK*.

A cock, going straight up, high, high, high. My gun goes up with him and is firm against my shoulder as he reaches the top of his leap. He seems to hang there as I fire, and he drops perfectly, two or three yards from where Moon waits.

"Good dog. Good boy, Moon," I say as he picks the heavy bird up in his mouth and brings it to me. "Moonie, that was perfect." The bird is thoroughly dead, but I open my pocket knife, press the blade into the roof of its mouth so that it will bleed properly. Check the spurs—they're stubby and almost rounded at the tip. This year's pheasant, probably. Young. Tender. Simply perfect.

Like a book pheasant, I think, and how seldom it happens. In the books, pheasants are said to rise straight up as this one did, going for altitude first, then pausing in the air to swing downwind. The books are quite wrong; most pheasants I see take straight off, without a jump, low and skimming, curving if they rise much, and never hanging at all. I wonder about evolution: among pheasant generations in this open country, did the ones who went towering into the air and hung like kites get killed off disproportionately? While the skulkers and skimmers and curvers survived, to transmit crafty genes?

"Old-fashioned pheasant, are you? You just set a record for me. I never dreamed I'd have a bird so early in the day." I check my watch.

9:03 Got a new device today ("Whoa, Moon. Wait, boy. Stay"), which may solve an old problem: how do you carry a pheasant?

They're big, chicken-size birds, with ten- to twenty-inch

[101]

tails. In the game-pocket of a hunting jacket the tail feathers break and the body plumage gets matted and unattractive; same goes for game bags. And I like to hang pheasants for a day or two on the screened back porch at home, as much to see them as to let them get high (I lack the courage to let a bird get very high)—anyway, this boy's for the freezer, to join the Christmas collection, young and plump as he is. And for the freezer, I don't hang them at all. In fact it would be best and easiest to pluck and draw him right now, in the field. But then I should have no pleasure at all of looking at him with my wife and children, something we all enjoy ritually:

"Get any, Daddy?" they will yell, running out of the house.

I have, almost every time I've gone out this year—generally no more than one—but there's still excitement. I will hold him up for them.

"Oh, isn't he beautiful."

"May I have the tail feathers? It's my turn."

Perhaps, I think as Moon and I reach the long grass, there'll be two sets of tail feathers today. Three? A limit? Limits are scarce this year, but perhaps, starting so well, so early . . .

9:15 The device I was so hopeful of is not working out too well. It is a leather holder which slides onto the belt, and has a set of rawhide loops. As I was supposed to, I have hooked the pheasant's legs into a loop, but he swings against my own leg at the knee. Maybe the thing was meant for taller men.

"Moon. This way. Come around, boy." I feel pretty strongly that we should hunt the edge.

The dangling bird is brushing grass tops. Maybe next time I should bring my trout creel, which is oversized, having been made by optimistic Italians. No half-dozen trout would much more than cover the bottom, but three cock pheasants might lie nicely in the willow, their tails extending backwards through the crack between lid and body, the rigidity of the thing protecting them as a game bag doesn't.

"Moon. Come back here. Come around." He hasn't settled down for the day. Old as he is, he still takes a wild run, first thing.

I'm pretty well settled, myself (it's that bird bumping against my leg). Now Moon does come back into the area I want him in, the edge between high grass and low; there's a distinction between following your dog when he's got something and trusting him to weigh odds. I know odds better, and here is one of those things that will be a cliché of hunting in a few years, since the game-management men are telling it to one another now and it's started filtering into outdoor magazines: the odds are that most game will be near the edge of cover, not in the center of it. The jargon phrase for this is "edge factor."

"Haven't you heard of the edge factor?" I yell at Moon. "Get out along the edge here, boy." And in a few steps he has a scent again. When he's got the tail factor going, the odds change, and I follow him, almost trotting to keep up, as he works from edge to center, back towards edge, after what must be a running bird. He slows a little, but doesn't stop; the scent is hot, but apparently the bird is still moving. Moon stops, points, holds. I walk as fast as I can, am in range—and Moon starts again. He is in a crouch now, creeping forward in his point. The unseen bird must be shifting; he is starting to run again, for Moon moves out of the point and starts to lope; I move, fast as I can and still stay collected enough to shoot—gun held in both hands out in front of me— exhilarated to see the wonderful mixture of exuberance and certainty with which Moon goes. To make such big happy moves, and none of them a false one, is something only the most extraordinary human athletes can do, after years of training—it comes naturally to almost any dog. And that pheasant out there in front of us—how he can go! Turn and twist through the tangle of stems, never showing himself, moving away from Moon's speed and my calculations. But we've got him—I think we do—Moon slows, points. Sometimes we win in a run down—usually not—usually the pheasant picks the right time, well out and away, to flush out of range— but this one stopped. Yes. Moon's holding again. I'm in range. I move up, beside the rigid dog. Past him. WHIRR-PT. The gun rises, checks itself, and I yell at Moon, who is ready to bound forward:

"Hen!"

Away she goes, and away goes Moon, and I yell: "Whoa. Hen, hen," but it doesn't stop him. He's pursuing, as if he could get up enough speed to rise into the air after her. "Whoa." It doesn't stop him. WHIRRUPFT. That stops him. Stops me too. A second hen. WHIRRUPFT. WHIRRUPFT. Two more. And another, that makes five who were sitting tight. And then, way out, far from this little group, through which he must have passed, and far from us, I see the cock, which is almost certainly the bird we were chasing (hens don't run like that), fly up silently, without a cackle, and glide away, across the road and out of sight.

9:30 "There's got to be another," I say to Moon. A man I know informed me quite vehemently a week ago that one ought never to talk to a dog in the field except to give commands; distracts him, the man said, keeps him too close. Tell you what, man: you run your dogs your way, and I'll run my dog mine. Okay?

We approach a fence, where the hayfield ends; the ground is clear for twenty feet before the fence line. Critical place. If birds have been moving ahead of us, and are reluctant to fly, this is where they'll hide. They won't run into the open. And just as I put this card in the calculator, one goes up, CUK CUK CUK, bursting past Moon full-speed and low, putting the dog between me and him so that, while my gun is ready, I can't shoot immediately; he rises only enough to clear the fence, sweeping left between two bushes as I fire, and I see the pellets agitate the leaves of the right-hand bush, and know I shot behind him.

Moon, in the immemorial way of bird dogs, looks back at me with what bird hunters who miss have immemorially taken for reproach.

We turn along the edge paralleling the fence. He may not have been the only one we chased down here—Moon is hunting, working from fence to edge, very deliberate. Me too. I wouldn't like to miss again. Moon swerves to the fence row, tries some likely brush. Nope. Lopes back to the edge, lopes along it. Point. Very stiff. Very sudden. Ten yards, straight ahead.

This is a beautifully awkward point, Moon's body curved into it, shoulders down, rear up, head almost looking back at me; this one really caught him. As now we'll catch the pheasant? So close. Dog so steady. I have the impression Moon's looking a bird straight in the eye. I move slowly. No need for speed, no reason to risk being off balance. Let's be so deliberate, so cool, so easy. The gun is ready to come up—I never have the feeling that I myself bring it up. Don't be off balance. He'll go now. Now. Nope—when he does, I try to tell myself, don't shoot too fast, let the bird get out a little, but I'm not really that good and confident in my shooting. Thanks be for brush loads. Ought to have them in both barrels for this situation. Will I have to kick the pheasant out? I am within two steps of Moon, who hasn't stirred except for the twitching of his shoulder and haunch muscles, when the creature bolts. Out he comes, under Moon's nose, and virtually between my legs if I didn't jump aside—a rabbit,

STAUNCH POINT
[105]

tearing for the fence row. I could recover and shoot, it's an easy shot, but not today; I smile, relax, and sweat flows. I am not that desperate for game yet.

I yell "Whoa" at Moon, and for some dog's reason he obeys this time. I should punish him, now; for pointing fur? But it's my fault—sometimes, being a one-dog man, I shoot fur over him, though I recognize it as a genuine error in bird-dog handling. But with the long bond of hunting and mutual training between us (for Moon trained me no less than I did him), my taking a rabbit over him from time to time—or a mongoose, or a kangaroo—is not going to change things between us.

In any case, my wife's never especially pleased to see me bring a rabbit home, though the kids and I like to eat them.

I smile, walking along, back to the car; the field is hunted out. Once she was pleased to see that kind of game. We were in Chile, and the money was running low. We were hanging on, watching it go down under the point where there was return fare for all of us; then a good deal lower than that. Waiting for a story to sell, writing letters to friends, hoping some one would have a couple of hundred to lend. Finally there were both a good friend (L.M.A., and thanks again) and a sale. But while both were pending, a Hungarian I knew in Santiago took me hunting, and I hope it's the only time I have to go when my gun is the difference between whether my kids have macaroni again for supper instead of meat. We were after anything—quail, doves, tinamou (the South American "partridge")—and had driven quite far from the city. Been run off one piece of open-looking land by a man on horseback with a rusty carbine, who said Don Pedro owned it; we had seen some quail out there, bobbing along —California quail, established in Chile about a hundred years ago—and argued a little. The man was perfectly polite; he agreed that it would be all right if we had permission from Don Pedro, but one would have to go to Paris for that. Don Pedro hadn't been in Chile since his early boyhood.

We found another place, an overgrown orchard that

must have been enormous once, and were hunting across it when this thing jumped up and started to run. I thought it was a stray dog, it was so large, and when the Hungarian shot, I thought: "The bastard, what's he doing?" Then he shot again, hit, but not squarely, and as the bounds the creature was making brought it in front of me I saw that it was a huge hare. My friend's shot had slowed it down; it was easy to hold on to the head and finish it. It was so big that, split in half, there was plenty in each half for a generous meal for each family. What hares!

I pat Moon, who whoaed for the rabbit. "Whoa, big babe," I say softly. "Whoasie-posner, whoa-daboodle-dog, big sweet posner baby dog..." I am rubbing his back. Not talk to your dog, for Christ-sake?

10:20 We are driving away from the hayfield. Three pheasants seen, two shot at, one hit. That's a good first hour. Damn good first hour. (But I should have had the other bird.)

10:25 Now I think as we drive: I spent a little more time there than I should have. Pacing is critical in bird hunting, much as it is in trout fishing: don't be hasty as long as there are good chances left, don't delay when the only chances left are poor ones. I always fish too slow, and never cover as much stream as I ought to.

10:30 I turn left, going in a general direction, waiting for a particular place to occur to me. As I drive along, I apply something a man who understands car-hunting told me once. His name is Culross, and he's one of those people who can't talk without teaching. But like a good teacher he knows his subject. I generally find him worth listening to:

"Car-hunting's just as much an art as any other kind," he said. "All right, it's an art for short-time hunters with sore feet. You live in the city, you're out of shape—hell, did you ever consider that being in shape's a privilege of the leisured, if your work's not physical? Huh?

"You got no places to hunt. When would you ever get out

around hunting cover? All you can do is drive around, Saturday afternoons, out where your presence is resented because you're a stranger—maybe even something terrible like a factory worker with a foreign name and a union card, huh? A communist, huh? Even a Democrat! The dirt roads are all you've got for hunting fields. And remember, there're other cars cruising with guys like you in them, looking for the same thing: a bird to bring home, so your stupid wife will shut up for once about how you should sell the gun you bought on payments through the classified.

"A leisured guy, with places to hunt, drives along a dirt road; if he glances at the ditch, he's looking for a pheasant. Not a real car-hunter—*he's* looking for small white rings. Just the little ring around the neck, huh? That's what shows up. All the rest is camouflaged. *You* might see your whole bird now and then, especially if it's moving. For every one you do, he'll see four or five, and most of them standing still. You oughta ride with one of these guys—they're amazing."

That was the opening of the lecture, and I'm a responsive student; white rings? I look for them, going along slowly, and after four or five minutes, I see one. It's in knee-high grass along some hog wire—the stuff that's woven in rectangles. Marking the fence post nearest the bird, I coast to a gradual stop, counting six more posts so I'll know where he was. I hoist myself in the seat and look back, through the rear window, to confirm that the cock is now indeed out of sight. I understand why the ring system works. To do a little lecturing myself—or perhaps write a footnote, since the information is from books—pheasants, where they're feeding or resting, raise their heads to look around two or three times each minute. It's a protective measure, of course, but it does bring the white ring out of cover.

Do I want to take this one? Moon is pawing at my shoulder, but he wouldn't be in on it. The situation would permit using the simplest of the three techniques my instructor described:

"Where there's a ditch on each side of the road, the car-hunter's got it made. We're talking about the legal car-hunter, huh? Illegally, he'd just have the shotgun ready, back up, and blast out the window into the grass.

"Legally, though. Say there's a fairly deep ditch on each side. He spots the post that marks the bird, pulls forward a little way, and gets out of his car on the far side from the pheasant. He crouches, and slips into that opposite ditch. Now he goes back down it, keeping low—he can't see the place where the bird is, but the bird can't see him either—and he counts till he's right across from the marked fence post. Okay. Now he turns, walks up on the road, straight toward the fence, and the first thing the pheasant knows, there's a man standing over him, fifteen yards away."

"I suppose the real sports sometimes even let the bird get up," I said.

"You think that's too easy? Sure they let him get up— and remember these guys aren't in a position to go out and shoot clay birds all year round. They don't have the time; they couldn't afford it. All right, here's another method. He carries a pistol. You know, this isn't illegal, huh? The law says you can't have a set-up gun in the car, but it doesn't cover pistols. You can have one, and have it loaded, lying on your lap. He stops right beside the bird, cuts the ignition to steady the car, aims down, right out the window—listen, it takes a pretty shot."

That was the second technique in the lecture. The third and most elaborate Virgil Culross called The Trojan Horse. This is used by men who don't own pistols, or who shoot them as badly as I do; it requires two men, and depends on the fact that pheasants are alarmed by persons but not by cars. It is used in situations where the ditches are too shallow for concealment, or where there is only one ditch, and may even work when there are no ditches at all. Having spotted and marked the bird, the Achilles of the pair gets out on the side opposite, shielded by the car, and loads up. Then the Ulysses slowly backs the car, Achilles walking along in concealment beside it. Just before the place where the pheasant is, Ulysses stops the Horse and Achilles strides forth.

I have been stopped long enough, going over my lecture notes and watching behind me, to have seen the white ring come up three more times. Now it comes up again. Moon bumps me, tries to push his eighty pounds across my lap and out the left front window—the only one open. I push him back. "To hell with it, Moon," I say. "Let's drop the course."

10:35 Another place has come to mind, a popcorn field on government land. I turn left, still following the same kind of fence which is characteristic of this area—three feet of hog wire at the bottom, and three stands of barbed wire above it.

In a way, the hog wire had as much to do with my deciding to let that roadside pheasant go as anything: about four years ago, when two or three pheasants a season was all I could manage, I jumped one who flew straight away from me into some hog wire and tried to squeeze through a rectangle; I shot him while he was tangled up. It was a mistake, given my rather intense feeling about shooting birds in the air—one of those mistakes which starts honest and turns dishonest: the pheasant seemed to be in flight at the beginning of the automatic sequence (mount gun, point, swing, fire) and it was nice of Mike Morgan, the man I was hunting with, to suggest that once the sequence is begun, one is hardly able to interrupt it. But it's not so; I interrupt it half a dozen times a day for hens. I knew that tangled bird was trapped, somehow or other, without registering just how, and fired anyway.

There are dirty memories in hunting, but wash them often enough in a fresh wind like today's, dry them in the sun, and they'll fade, and shrink and sometimes even take on another color:

"There's one," Aroldo said, in Spanish. We were bumping along a terrible Uruguayan road. It was mid-afternoon and pleasantly cool.

Reuben stopped the jeep.

"Watch," Reuben told me. I was sitting in back. "In a moment he will put up his head again."

"It's better on horseback, or a bicycle," Aroldo said, staring intently at a spot of pampas grass. He had a stronger Uruguayan accent than did Reuben, who was educated and had traveled in Spain. "You go slower and see more."

Then I saw the bird's head come up, a small head on a long, thin neck and, stunning me a little because it was just behind me and unexpected, Aroldo fired and smashed the bird. The gun was of some small bore, not much larger than a .410. It was Reuben's gun as a matter of fact. Reuben was going to shoot my wife's 20-gauge.

"A bad shot," Aroldo said, hopping out. "I meant only to shoot the head off."

When he returned with the bird and handed it to me to look at—I had never seen a tinamou before—I said, trying to be tactful: "With a larger gun, would you get out and make the bird fly before you shot?"

Reuben seemed to think that was an interesting idea. Aroldo, who was a mechanic with five boys to feed, took it for a joke. Or was it my difficulty with Spanish tenses?

There are two ways to approach the popcorn field. I pause at the country schoolhouse, where I could go straight or turn left, and decide that the place I should start hunting, to take advantage of wind direction, will be more quickly reached if I go straight. The day has brightened up a lot, and the wind is a little calmer. The high corn still waves, but its rustling is soft now, unlike the sighing and cracking that the stalks were making in the cornfield across from where I started. Decision made, I start again.

I had eaten tinamou, and seen pictures, but the bird was a surprise. He was half again the size of a quail, long-necked and meaty looking, brown all over. He was virtually tailless, a little cousin of the South American ostrich. I wondered whether he could be much of a flyer. He's the one called *perdiz*, Spanish for partridge.

A few minutes later, Aroldo spotted another by the roadside—what roadhunter's eyes he had, with not even a white ring to look for—and it was to be my bird; he was on the left. I was sitting on the right of the jeep, Aroldo in back. Reuben, in the driver's seat, smiled and watched to see what I would do.

I got out on the right side, loaded my gun, and Aroldo said: "Across the car. Shoot over the radiator." But I walked around behind the jeep, my gun ready, looking, trying to spot the tinamou. Aroldo shifted to the side of the back seat nearest me and pointed. "There. Right in there, beside the stone."

I saw the head come up and look directly at me. "Shoot. Shoot, Señor."

I waited. I stamped my foot as hard as I could, recalling how impact on the ground will sometimes flush a pheasant, and the tinamou went. I mounted the gun, and it reached my right shoulder about the time Aroldo's hand reached my left.

"Too late, too late, Señor," Aroldo cried, exasperated, pulling at me to prevent my wasting a shell. "Can't you see the partridge is flying?"

Much of a flyer? I'd never seen anything go so fast. Moon knows landmarks, I'm convinced, even before we get to a place. He sees that we are not far, now, from the place where we left the car to hunt the popcorn field two days ago, and he begins pacing back and forth on the back seat, as caged hunting animals do in zoos.

"I'm thinking about you, Moon," I say. "Remember Reuben?" I rub his shoulder roughly, trying to calm him down.

Moon was some use on tinamou, though as with pheasants, a pointing dog who ranges will show you a good many more birds than you'll get close to. Tinamou are thoroughly unpredictable—sometimes they lie, sometimes they run. At any rate he got shots for Reuben and me both, when we were finally out of the jeep to hunt through a grassy field. Aroldo, roadhunter and pot-shooter to the end, refused to try this nonsensical way of hunting, but he followed in order to watch the clowns. He and Reuben had been arguing, in Spanish too rapid for me to follow, about whether the way I claimed to shoot was feasible. Now, as Moon found, chased, and flushed a bird, I was feeling the discomfort of being the subject of an argument, who must demonstrate which contender is correct about him; it was a kind of pressure to which I reacted miserably. The bird went straightaway, at that wild speed, and I missed completely with both barrels. There was another bird a moment later, which seemed to me

Reuben's shot, but he was apparently more interested in winning the debate than in shooting the bird. By the time I realized that he wanted me to shoot again, the bird was too far out and I missed again; I shouldn't have tried.

But then the next tinamou, oh boy, the next one. Moon raised it right at Reuben's feet, and it flew left, the far side from me, so that there was no question of my shooting at it. And damned if Reuben didn't take an instant to look over, smile, and say:

"All right now?" And then swing back beautifully and stop it dead in the air, thirty yards away.

I liked Reuben. He helped manage a hotel out in the country, was a fine big-game fisherman and a natural at doing things well out of doors—a slight, compact, graceful man, with real elegance of movement and of mind as well.

I missed two more birds (they really do go like hell). Reuben missed one, and hit another. Aroldo got bored, and turned back to the car to wait for us to be ready to resume roadhunting, when I redeemed myself. The tinamou came from the right at full speed, twenty-five yards out, and right across the sun which was forty-five degrees past zenith; I had the gun on him just before he disappeared completely in glare, fired anyway, and could hardly believe it when he came falling out of the blaze.

I'm not sure Aroldo ever did believe I'd made the shot, and I minded then; but memories change color, and now I feel it was Reuben I wanted to make it for, anyway.

I am still thinking about tinamou and still watching the ditch as we come in sight of the place where I will park to go to the popcorn field. They're a marvelous bird, very much like pheasants in their ways, and I wonder whether anyone has ever thought of trying to establish them in the South of this country where pheasants won't take. I still watch the Iowa ditch, go by a little stand of wild plum and then some bottle gentian, bemused with wondering how I would feel if, instead of a white ring, I should see the long neck and bright eyes of a tinamou look out from under it.

10:40 Step out of the car, look around, work it out: the birds slept late this morning, because of the wind and frost, and may therefore be feeding late. If so, they're in the field itself, which lies beyond two fallow fields. They roost here in this heavy cover, fly out to the corn—early on nice mornings; later, if I'm correct, on a day like this. When they're done feeding, they go to what game experts call loafing cover—relatively thin cover, near the feeding place, and stay in it till the second feeding in the afternoon; after which they'll be back here where they started, to roost again.

The wind is on my left cheek, as Moon and I go through the roosting cover, so I angle right. This will bring us to where we can turn and cross the popcorn field, walking straight into the wind. This will not only be better for Moon, for obvious reasons, but will also be better for shooting; birds in open rows, hearing us coming, can sail away out of range very fast with the wind behind them. If it blows towards me, they'll either be lifted high, going into the wind, or curve off to one side or the other.

Am I actually rehearsing all this bookish stuff, so consciously? Yes, I observe, watching myself rehearse bookish stuff, as I follow easily along after Moon, who is hunting easily; we're in our all-day stride, now, a fast enough pace but not tiring, settled but strong—it takes a week or two of daily hunting before I can move like this. The bookish stuff leaves my head gradually, as we go along, not in a straight line—checking a little piece of cover here, trying the fence row for a way. Finally the rhythm of the walking, the weight of the gun, the continuous, rapid yet strangely minute scanning of the ground in front and to the sides, makes what I am doing as completely physical—non-mental—as what Moon does as he lopes, letting his nose tell him where to turn. I could not explain, if someone were with me, why I leave the good-looking fence row which Moon still follows, and cut left, out of my general line of walking—and I wouldn't want to pause to justify it. It's simply that I know, gradually, where a pheasant is.

Moon knows, too. I've barely made my first step when he swerves off his line, and takes a parallel to the way I'm going now—towards a small draw that I'd never noticed before in this field, a place that may be just a little swampy when it's rainy, a place with a stand of giant ragweed growing in it. There's no need to control the dog; the harmony with which we hunt together when we're working right is all established for today, though I couldn't say just when it started being so. He won't waste my steps or his own—what is it they say of thirty-five-year-old infielders? He can still cover the position but he doesn't take the extra step any longer? Something like that; but in dog terms, Moon is still playing second base in his fifties.

The ragweed, as we come up close to it and Moon pauses before choosing a spot at which to plunge in, is eight feet high—thick, dry, brittle, grey-stemmed stuff which pops and crackles as he breaks into it. I move a few feet along the edge of the draw, shifting my position as I hear him working through, to stay as well in range of where he is as possible. I am calmly certain there's a bird in there, even that it's a cock. I think he moved in ahead of us as we were coming up the field, felt safe when he saw us apparently about to pass by, and doesn't want to leave the dense overhead protection now.

But he must. Moon will send him up in a moment, perhaps out the far side where the range will be extreme. It will be a long shot, if that happens, and Moon is now at the far edge, is turning along it, when I hear the cackle of the cock rising. For a moment I don't know where, can't see him, and by the time I do he's going out to my right, almost back towards me, having doubled away from the dog. Out he comes, already in full flight and low, with the wind behind him for speed. And yet I was so well set for this, for anything, that it all seems easy—to pivot, mounting the gun as I do, find it against my cheek and the bird big and solid at the end of the barrel, swing, taking my time, and shoot. The bird checks, fights air, and tumbles, and in my sense of perfection I make an error: I am so sure he's perfectly hit that I do not take the second shot, before he falls in some waist-high weeds. I mark the place by keeping my eye on a particular weed, a little taller than the others, and walk slowly, straight towards it, not letting my eye move away, confident he'll be lying right

[115]

by it. Moon, working the ragweed, would neither see the rise nor mark the fall and he comes bounding out to me now, coming to the sound of the shot. I reach the spot first, so very carefully marked, and there's no bird there. I feel a small, familiar panic. I put an empty shell case over the top of the particular weed on which I was holding my eye, as Moon comes to the place, snuffles excitedly, proving that the bird did land exactly here. And then, of course, the pheasant must have run.

Hunters make errors; dogs correct them. While I am still standing there, irritated with myself for not having shot twice, Moon is circling me, casting, inhaling those great snuffs, finding the ground scent. He begins to work a straight line, checks as I follow him, starts again in a slightly different direction; I must trust him, absolutely, and I do. I remind myself that once he trailed a crippled bird more than half a mile in the direction opposite from that in which I had actually seen the bird start off. I kept trying to get him to go the other way, but he wouldn't; and he found the pheasant. It was by the edge of a dirt road, so that Max Morgan and I could clock the distance afterwards by car speedometer.

Our present bird is no such problem. Forty feet from where the empty shell waves gently back and forth on top of the weed, Moon hesitates, points. Then, and I do not know how he knows that this particular immobile pheasant will not fly (unless it's the smell of fresh blood), Moon lunges. His head darts into matted weeds, fights spurs for a moment, tosses the big bird once so that he can take it by the back, lifts it; and he comes to me proudly, trotting, head as high as he can hold it.

I accept the bird, grasping the legs; kill it with my knife and look at the spurs. They are like locust thorns, but tougher—sharp, well over an inch in length.

"You weren't where you were supposed to be, were you?" I say to dead bird. "The books said you wouldn't be here near the roost. You were supposed to be feeding or loafing or something." I decide that the cold weather must have brought him back to heavy cover, after his morning feed.

[116]

11:00 Iowa hunters are obsessed with corn. If there are no birds in the cornfields, they consider the situation hopeless. This may come from the fact that most of them hunt in drives —a number of men spread out in line, going along abreast through standing corn, with others blocking the end of the field. My experience, for I avoid that kind of hunt every chance I get, is quite different; I rarely find pheasants in cornfields, except along the edges. More than half of those I shoot, I find away from corn, in wild cover, and sometimes the crops show that the bird has not been eating grain at all but getting along on wilder seeds.

But as I start to hunt the popcorn field, something happens that shows why driving often works out. We start into the wind, as planned, moving down the field the long way, and way down at the other end a farm dog sees us. He starts towards us, intending to investigate Moon, I suppose. I see him come towards the field; I see him enter it, trotting our way, and the wind carries the sound of his barking. And then I see—the length of a football field away, reacting to the farm dog—pheasants go up; not two or three, but a flock, twelve or fourteen, and another and another and another, cocks and hens, flying off in all directions, sailing down wind and out of sight. Drivers and blockers would have had fast shooting with that bunch—but suppose I'd got up? Well, this gun only shoots twice. And, well again, boy. Three's the limit, dunghead. And you've got two already.

11:30 Two birds before lunch? I ought to limit out, I ought to limit out soon. And stop looking for pheasants, spend the afternoon on something else. Take Moon home to rest, maybe, and know that the wind's going down and the sun's getting hot, go into the woods for squirrels, something I like but never get around to.

Let's get the other one. Where?

We are walking back to the car, the shortest way, no reason to go through the popcorn field after what happened. Where? And I think of a pretty place, not far away.

11:45 Yes, it's pretty. Got a bird here last year, missed a couple, too, why haven't I been here this season? It's a puzzle, and the solution, as I stop the car once more, is a pleasure: I know a lot of pretty places near home, twenty or thirty of them, all quite distinct, and have gotten or missed birds at all of them, one season or another.

This place I enter just as I did a year ago, finding a special contentment in the way the land has waited for me to come back, without changing. I go in along a little creek, with a soybean field at one side—someone's corn lies on the other side, but that land is private. I remember an old tree, lying across the stream, where I jumped a wood-duck unexpectedly last year, and would hardly be surprised if the same duck jumped again. Behind the soybean field, and still along the creek, lies a swampy meadow which is where the three pheasants were, the ones I missed and the one I hit. As I come into the meadow, I think the young soft maples are a little taller, the swampy part a little drier. But the birds I missed were both along the edges of the swampy ground, in thick marsh grass. Moon starts around it clockwise, and almost superstitiously, I call him back to circle it the other way, just as we did last year.

There are no pheasants this time, only signs of pheasant; roosting places, full of droppings. Some fresh enough so that they were dropped this morning. A place for the next windy morning; I put that idea in a safe place, and move back, after Moon—he's pretty excited with all the bird scent, but not violently; it's not that fresh—towards the fence along the soybean field. We turn from the creek, and go along the fence line, twenty or thirty feet out, towards an eight-acre patch of woods where I have often seen deer, and if I were a real reasoner or a real instinct man, not something in between, what happens would not find me unprepared. Moon goes into a majestically rigid point, foreleg raised, tail out straight, aimed at low bushes in the fence row. I hardly ever see him point so rigidly without first showing the signs he gives while the quarry is still shifting. I move in rather casually, suspecting a hen, but if it's a cock rather confident, after my last great shot, and there suddenly comes at me, buzzing angrily, a swarm of—pheasants? Too small—hornets? Sparrows?

Quail! drilling right at me, the air full of them, whirring, swerving to both sides.

Much too late, surprised, confused—abashed, for this is classic quail cover—I flounder around, face back the way I came, and pop off a pair of harmless shots, more in valediction than in hope of hitting. Turn back to look at Moon, and up comes a straggler, whirring all by himself, also past me. There are no easy shots on quail, but I could have him, I think, if both barrels weren't empty. He's so close that I can see the white on neck and face, and know him for a male. Jock though I am, at least I mark him down, relieved that he doesn't cross the creek.

And neither, so shows an image unremarked at the time of shooting but now readily enough recalled, did the main bunch. Hell, I think, they didn't fly far. This covey hasn't been hunted—they're scattered out, right in front of us between here and the creek, and I've got one marked to start on. Moon, as a matter of fact, has already started on him, started casting for singles, and I almost forget to reload in my eagerness to get over to him. But I stop and make myself be deliberate: brush loads in both barrels, walk carefully, stay alert. How many times a season must I remind myself that there is one first law of hunting: always be ready to shoot?

Moon, working with cautious excitement out ahead, has already made the decision I'd have hesitated over—go right in after a covey rises, or let them settle? I've been with experienced quail hunters who did both; well, I could call Moon back—he *might* come. (If it were a marked down pheasant, my own experience would tell me what to do: since he'd land running, the best chance of finding him would be to circle way beyond the landing place, hoping he'd have had cause to stop, and then hunt back towards it—otherwise I'd never overcome his lead.) Okay. Let Moon decide this one.

Moon works straight to the spot where I marked the straggler, and sure enough he flushes, not giving the dog a chance to point, flushes high and I snap-shoot and he falls. Moon bounds after him and stops on the way, almost pitching forward, like a car when its brakes lock. Another bird. Ready. I hope I have my down bird marked. Careful. *Whirrr*—I damn near stepped on him, and back he goes behind me. I swing 180 degrees, and as he angles away have him over the end of the barrel. As I fire, it seems almost accidental that I should be on him so readily, but it's not of course—it's the one kind of shot that never misses, the unplanned, reflexive shot, when conditioning has already operated before self-consciousness could start up. This quail falls in the soft maple seedlings, in a place I won't forget, but the first one may be hard.

He's not. I find him without difficulty, seeing him on the ground at just about the same time that Moon finds him too. Happy to have him, I bring Moon back to the soft maple seedlings, but we do not find the second bird.

We hunt and hunt. After five or ten minutes, there is not enough scent left to keep Moon interested, and I suppose the bird dead long enough now so that the body heat—and the scent with it?—is mostly gone. I comb through the maple seedlings for twenty minutes more. It seems to me terrible to lose a bird. I walk back to where I stood to make the shot, and look down again. I walk directly back to where I have just spent half an hour hunting—Moon is off digging in some soft earth—and there, where I must have looked a dozen times, lies my second quail.

"It's good to see you," I say, enormously relieved.

When I was a child I never paid much attention to conventional superstitions; I was always too busy making up my own as I went along. I revert to this, rather gravely informing myself that, since I have exceeded my luck in finding this lost bird, I am not to hunt the other singles.

I call Moon, and we walk back to the car. It was a small covey anyway; quail are scarce after the bitter winter last year. Let the tribe increase.

12:30 Lunch is black coffee in the thermos, an apple and an orange, and the sight of two quail and two pheasants, lying in a neat row on the car floor. I had planned to go home for lunch; and it wouldn't take so very much time; but I would talk with my family, of course, and whatever it is this noon that they're concerned with, I would be concerned with. And that would break the spell, as an apple and an orange will not.

12:45 Also

1:45 and, I'm afraid,

2:45 these hours repeat one another, and at the end of them I have: two pheasants, as before; two quail; and an afterthought.

The afterthought shouldn't have run through my mind, in the irritable state that it was in.

During each hour I hunted hard, through good pheasant cover: first, a couple of acres of smartweed, crisscrossing it thoroughly, where two hens were. Then an abandoned lane, grassy and promising, between two cornfields and out into the meadow past the lane, where no birds were at all. And finally, a cornfield belonging to a man from whom I have general permission. This looked magnificent. Half the corn was picked, so that blocks of stubble twelve rows wide alternated with blocks of standing corn the same width. No pheasants.

The only shots I took were at domestic pigeons, going by fast and far up, considered a nuisance around here; I missed both times. But what made me irritable were all the mourning doves.

There are doves all over the place in Iowa, in every covert that I hunt—according to the last Audubon Society spring census at Des Moines, doves were more common even than robins and meadow larks. In my three hard hours of barren pheasant hunting, I could have had shots at twenty or twenty-five doves (a game bird in thirty states, a game bird throughout the history of the world), and may not try them. Shooting doves is against the law in Iowa. The harvesting of our enormous surplus (for nine out of ten will die before they're a year old anyway) is left to cats and owls and—because the dove ranges get so crowded—germs.

Leaving the half-picked cornfield, I jump yet another pair of doves, throw up my gun and track them making a pretended double, though I doubt that it would work.

Leaving Uruguay, we were driving across Argentina, going to Chile on the main road, the only road, I guess.

Late in the afternoon of the second day we stopped to rest the children and run the dog at a place where the shoulders of the road were wide and grassy and shaded by rows of trees. There were grainfields on the left, wheat I think, and there must have been water somewhere out to the right, for as we rested on the grass, doves starting coming over from the grain, in small flocks, like blackbirds.

My wife said, "Sure. Why don't we?" and I got our shotguns from the car, smiling and excited for the first time in what had been a hot and wearing day. Each of us picked a tree to stand behind—twenty feet out behind it so that we'd be clear of branches overhead; three times I missed as doves came over my tree, and the fourth, firing again at the lead bird of a flock, I saw the fifth in line fold its wings and come diving down, dead at my feet. I was amazed. I'd had no idea such speed and such leading were involved.

"Try about a six-length lead," I called to my wife, picking up the dove and finding it well hit, which showed that the full pellet pattern had reached it—not simply a stray one. Up to that moment neither of us had hit.

My wife lowered her gun. "That's impossible."

"It's true. They're that fast."

"I don't mean impossible for doves. I mean impossible for me," she said. She took one more shot, into the middle of a tight flock she said, and a bird fell. She brought it to me, smiling, and said: "There's no sense doing it that way, is there?" She took her gun apart, cased it, and went over to play with the children.

I tried that unbelievable lead, shooting at rear birds now as they passed over so as to be sure of which one I was pointing at, and twelve or fourteen shots later, had six more doves. That made eight, so I stopped, rather reluctantly: two each. After the food of hot roadside restaurants, the doves were marvelous, drawn and toasted on sticks over a little outdoor fire.

"I'll know how to get them in Illinois now," I boasted.

"If we ever get back." What dove shooting we do from

Iowa must be done across the border. But to know a lead in theory is far different from having it automatically, out at the end of the moving arc projected from your eye along a shotgun barrel. And doves once shot at, as the Argentine ones had probably not been, learn to swerve and change speed—in Illinois, since we've been back, I still miss far more than I hit.

Three hours of seeing doves, and no pheasants, has made me pettish, and perhaps I am beginning to tire.

Pettishly I think about company for dinner tomorrow night: we can't serve the two pheasants that I have together, really, for one is big and mature and should be stewed. It would be indecent to do anything but roast or broil the other —anyway, I need him for the Christmas collection.

A rabbit jumps out behind the dog, unseen by Moon but not by me. At first I assume that I want to let him go, as I did the earlier one; then he becomes the afterthought: company, dinner—so you won't let me shoot doves, eh rabbit? He's dead before he can reach cover.

Moon checks, comes back; I race him to the rabbit, and wrestle him for it. Moon has to let me win the tug of war so he sits, like a little dog doing a trick, and watches while I field-dress the animal, skinning and drawing. Moon is fairly sure that, when I get to them, I will give him fresh heart and bloody liver—damn dog licks his lips. Actually, I lick mine, too: there's a jointed squirrel still left in the freezer. Squirrel and jointed rabbit and the big pheasant, browned and then stewed together slowly in a casserole; onion and tomato and parsley and garlic and carrots in the stock; shelled corn and lima beans added in the final minutes so they won't overcook . . . "When do you put the wine in?" I asked my wife once.

"Some at first to flavor the stock," she said. "Some at the end to flavor the stew, and the rest on the table to flavor the guests."

3:00 Now I have only an hour left to get my final bird, for pheasant hunting ends at four. This is a symbolic bird: a good hunter gets his limit. At noon it seemed almost sure I would; suddenly it's doubtful.

I sit in the car, one hand on Moon who is lying on the seat beside me. We've reached the time of the day when he rests when he can.

There are a couple of likely places near here, farm land where I could probably get permission if I asked, but I hate asking permission. It's not being refused—people know me around here so that I seldom am—nor will I go on private land without it. But the asking, as Henry Akers once said, is too much like going up and ringing a stranger's bell and trying to sell insurance. Generally, too, the farmer himself isn't around. (A man will almost always say okay.) You look hopefully around the barn, but he's not in sight. A dog barks or growls as you go into the yard. If you can get by him, and reach the doorbell, odds are there's no one home to answer. If there is, it's generally the farm wife. And she is perfectly pleasant, but she doesn't really know if it's all right or not—it's her husband's function to give permission to hunt, not hers.

Once, going out with the volunteer fire department from town, I helped put out a hoghouse fire on a farm near here, and have often driven past it since and noticed how good the cover looks. They might not remember me from the fire, but if I reminded them, then surely . . . ? I haven't the stomach for it. I think of my great luck in having so much open land to hunt; I know that elsewhere in the country such freedom grows more and more uncommon. Signs are going up. Farms posted, or subdivided. Commercial shooting places taking over, where hunting is by fee, with planted birds. I can't imagine where the pleasure is in that. Then, if we move to such an area, must I give up hunting?

(No. I shall buy my own acres—I give myself this out as I start the car again, turn around, and head away down the road to a place I have thought of. And I shall put up a fence twelve feet high. And signs, saying:

> KEEP THE HELL
> AWAY FROM HERE,
> BOY.

KILLER
DOGS

IMPORTED
CROCODILES

RADIATION

BEWARE THE VICIOUS BASTARD, ME

in letters tall enough to be read from two miles off.)

3:10 On my way to someplace else, I suddenly brake the car. "Hey, did you see that?" I am talking to Moon again. He has a paw over his nose, and of course saw nothing. I look over him, eagerly, out the window and down into a big marsh we were about to pass by. We were on our way to the place I'd thought of, an old windbreak of evergreens near an abandoned farmhouse site, surrounded by overgrown pasture, and not too far from corn. It's an ace-in-the-hole kind of place for evening shooting, for the pheasants come in there early to roost; I've used it sparingly, shown it to no one.

Going there would be our best chance to fill out, I think, but look: "Damn, Moon, snipe. Snipe, boy, I'm sure of it."

On the big marsh, shore birds are rising up and setting down, not in little squadrons like kildeer—which are shore birds about the same size, and very common—but a bird here, a bird there. Becoming instantly invisible when they land, too, and so not among the wading shore birds. I get out the glasses and step out of the car, telling Moon to stay. I catch one of the birds in the lenses, and the silhouette is unmistakable—the long, comic beak, the swept-back wings.

"You are snipe," I say, addressing—well, them, I suppose. "Where've you boys been?"

Two more whiz in and out of the image, too quickly to follow, two more of my favorite of all game birds. Habitat changes around here so much from year to year, with the great

[125]

fluctuations in water level from the dam, that this marsh, which was full of snipe three years ago, has shown none at all so far this year. What snipe hunting I've found has been in temporarily puddled fields, after rains, and in a smaller marsh.

"I thought you'd never come," I say. "Moon!" I open the car door. "Moon, let's go." My heartiness is a little false, for snipe are my favorite bird, not Moon's. He'll flush them, if he must, but apparently they're distasteful to him, and when I manage to shoot one, he generally refuses even to pick it up, much less retrieve it for me.

Manage to shoot one? Last year, on the first day I hunted snipe, I shot sixteen shells before I hit my first. That third pheasant can wait there in the hole with the other aces.

Remembering the sixteen straight misses, I stuff my pockets with shells—brush loads still for the first shot but, with splendid consistency, high-brass 7½'s for the second, full-choke shot. I won't use them on a big bird, like a pheasant; I will on a tiny bird, like a snipe. The snipe goes fast, and by the second shot you need all the range you can get.

I should have hip boots now. Go back home and get them? Nuts. Get muddy.

Down we go, Moon with a certain silly enthusiasm for the muskrats he smells and may suppose are now to be our quarry. I see that the marsh water is shallow, but the mud under it is always deep—thigh-deep in some places; the only way to go into it is from hummock to hummock of marsh grass. Actually, I will stay out of it if I can, and so I turn along the edge, Moon hunting out in front. A snipe rises over the marsh at my right, too far to shoot at, scolding us anyway: *scaip, scaip*. Then two more, which let the dog get by them, going up between me and Moon—a chance for a double, in a highly theoretical way. I shoot and miss at the one on the left as he twists low along the edge. He rises, just after the shot, going up in a tight turn, and I shoot again, swinging up with him, and miss again. And grin. This is snipe hunting.

At my first shot, the other snipe—the one I didn't shoot at—dove, as if hit. But I know he wasn't; I've seen the trick before. I know about where he went in, and I decide not to bother with Moon, who is chasing around in the mud, trying

SMART RETRIEVE (I)

to convince himself that I knocked down a pheasant or something decent like that.

I wade in myself, mud to ankles, mud to calves, mud to the tops of the low boots I'm wearing; no bird? What the hell, mud over the boot tops, and I finally climb a hummock. This puts up my diving snipe, ten yards further out and scolding, but the hummocks are spaced too far apart in this part of the swamp so there's no point shooting. I couldn't recover him and I doubt that Moon would. I let him rise, twist, swoop upwards, and I stand as still as I can, balanced on the little mound of grass; I know a trick myself. It works; at the top of his climb the snipe turns and comes streaking back, forty yards up, directly overhead. I throw up the gun for the fast overhead shot, and miss. Grin—yes, I do. Missing snipe doesn't depress me, as missing any other kind of bird does. There are two reasons: everybody misses snipe. And if you've

[127]

found them at all, you've generally found a fair-sized group of them and will be shooting for a while.

I splash back to the edge and muck along. A snipe goes up, almost at my feet, and his first swerve coincides with my snap shot—a kind of luck that almost seems like skill. Moon, bounding back, has seen the bird fall and runs to it—smells it, curls his lip and slinks away. He turns his head to watch me bend to pick it up, and as I do, leaps back and tries to take it from me.

"Moondog," I say, addressing him severely by his full name. "I'm not your child to punish. I like this bird. Now stop it."

We start along again, come to the corner where the marsh dries out, and turn. Moon stops, sight-pointing in a half-hearted way, and a snipe goes up in front of him. This one curves towards some high weeds; I fire and miss, but stay on him as he suddenly straightens and goes winging straight out, rising very little. He is a good forty yards away by now, but he tumbles when I fire, and falls on open ground. It takes very little to kill a snipe. I pace the distance, going to him, and watch Moon, for Moon picks this one up. Then, when I call to him to bring it, he gradually, perhaps sulkily, lowers his head and spits it out again. He strolls off as if there were nothing there. I scold him as I come up, but not very hard; he looks abashed, and makes a small show of hunting dead in a bare spot about ten yards from where we both know the snipe is lying. I pick up the bird, and tell Moon that he is probably the worst dog that ever lived, but not in an unkind voice for I wouldn't want to hurt his feelings.

This is a pleasanter area we are crossing now: firm mud, patches of swamp weeds, frequent puddles. Moon, loping around aimlessly, blunders into a group of five or six snipe at the far side of a puddle, and I put trying to get a double out of my mind; I try to take my time, pick out an individual, follow him as he glides towards some high reeds and drop him. I wonder if I ever hit two snipe on consecutive shots before.

Now we go along, towards the back of the marsh, shooting and missing, hitting just twice. One shot in particular pleases me: a snipe quite high, in full flight coming towards me. I shoot, remembering a phrase I once read: "A shotgun is a paint brush." I paint the snipe blue, to match the sky, starting my brush stroke just behind him, painting evenly along his body, completing the stroke about three lengths in front where I fire, and follow through. This is a classic shot, a memorable one, so much so that there are just two others I can put with it—one on a faraway pheasant last year, one on a high teal in Chile. The sky is all blue now, for the snipe is painted out of it and falls, almost into my hand.

I have five, and with them a stirring of aspiration. It never seemed possible before that I might someday shoot a limit of snipe, yet a limit is only eight—just three more. They are pretty well gone from the marsh, except for the end where the mud would be too much for me. I turn and hunt my way out of the marsh, then go along a shallow watercourse, into a wet field. A snipe goes up from just beside the water, and just out of range. Moon must stay in close, now, where is he?

"Moon? Moon?"

The dog is over to the left, unmoving—on point! For a snipe? Silently, slowly, almost majestically, a cock pheasant rises from the thick dry grass, without a cackle. The gun is with him, infinitely deliberate—he is too easy, almost, for an eye speeded up to the verve and size of snipe. I hold on him forever, shoot with a certain tenderness, and it seems that even his fall is as slow as it is certain.

It is just 3:55.

There is magic in this. The end of the legal pheasant hunting day is four o'clock.

4:00 Just after the pheasant, I kill another snipe, the sixth. He is along the stream, too, and so I follow it, awed at the thought that I might even get a limit of these. But on the next chance, not a hard one, I think too hard, and miss the first shot, as he twists, and the rising one as well.

We continue to hunt through the wet field and Moon puts up a small duck, a gadwall I think, but it's in the setting sun and might as easily be a small hen mallard. In easy range, but I'm not hunting ducks this year—look, look at her: Only one duck in a place like this, this perfect habitat?

We leave the watercourse for a tiny marsh, go back to it (or a branch) through government fields I've never crossed before, by strange potholes and unfamiliar willow stands. We flush a woodcock, cousin to the snipe, but shooting him is not permitted here. We turn away in a new direction—snipe and woodcock favor different sorts of cover. And sometime along in there, I walk up two snipe, shoot one very fast, and miss a perplexing but not impossible shot at the other, as he spirals up.

"There he goes," I think. "My limit bird." He flies into the east, where the sky is getting dark; clouds have come to the western horizon and the sun is gone for the day, behind them.

4:55 Ten minutes now till sunset, when snipe must be left to rest, and I go carefully, hoping for one more. Five ducks overhead, wood ducks going to roost; but there should be swarms.

"Try the bañado," Aroldo said. "Any time of day."

"Afternoon is better," Reuben said. "Or very early morning."

"At home we get up for ducks when it's still dark," I told them.

That afternoon I got seven ducks: in local nomenclature they were a *chiflon*, a *colorado*, a pair of *picazos*, and three *overos*. The *chiflon* I took just after I reached the bañado, a place half lake, half swamp, before I had really settled myself to hunting. There is a causeway through the place, and I had just stepped onto it, and was looking at some birds I thought might be gallinules along the edge; as I turned, a beautiful, small duck hurled itself out of the water and crossed the causeway just in front of me, its wings flashing an intense, electric green. I shot in surprise, very quickly, and when he dropped was equally astonished. It was difficult to get birds identified in Uruguay—one's curiosity about it was even considered a little eccentric—but I finally put him down as a Lesser Brazilian Teak.

The *colorado* was also on the water beside the causeway. He flushed and flew off low, right along the surface, following the causeway edge, and was not a hard shot. I had missed several like him and hit a couple, so I knew what he was already—an Argentine Cinamon Teal.

On the far side of the causeway I went off into the reeds and hid, and it was there I finally took the *picazos*— I cannot say what the several kinds may have been that I missed. The *picazos*—I shot them as a double, which is very rare for me—were a pair, male and female, huge black ducks of the pochard family which includes our canvasbacks. In English they are called Rosybills, though actually the female's bill is blue.

But the *overos*: when I left for South America, there was a phrase in my mind, a bird name. I can't even tell you why, though I know it came from looking through *Wildfowl of the World,* that great, inaccessibly expensive, three-volume compilation illustrated by Peter Scott, of which all I shall ever be able to afford is the very valuable little paperbound *Color Key,* in which Scott's paintings are reproduced in miniature and from which I made all my eventual identifications. In any case, my bird name, which became one of those romantic, echo phrases, and stood foɪ all the wild South American nature I hoped to see, was The Chiloe Widgeon.

My favorite of the fourteen kinds of unfamiliar duck I shot in Uruguay was the *pato overo,* and oddly enough, Chiloe Widgeons is just what they turned out to be. I found them generally in fields—the afternoon in the bañado they were in the pasture behind my blind of reeds, in a group of six or eight. I liked them because one could miss the jump shot, precisely as I did that day, and have a second chance, for they came back, wheeling around and around the field as I crouched, not even very well concealed. I shot my three birds that way—they are lovely, with black-and-white wings, white patched faces, and bright red-brown streaks along the belly; and they are marvelous ducks for the table, Chiloe Widgeons are: I wish I'd known they were what I was shooting at the time, rather than finding out, as I did, by looking them up when I got back home.

The pampas sky, as I picked up my *overos* that evening, was gradually filling with water fowl on their way to the bañado, and I went back to my hiding place in the reeds to see the sight. They were coming in, all right, waves of them: great flights of snow-white geese, and of swans with black necks; cormorants and clouds of shore birds. A huge rail (I guess) ran close to me and disappeared in some tall grass, a rail bigger than a chicken. Phalaropes, or so I think they were, came swimming out in front. And the ducks were myriad.

I had no impulse to shoot. Seven ducks seemed a decent number—enough for my family, for Reuben and his brother, a couple for Aroldo. But even if I'd had none, I don't think I would have shot, for I did not want to interrupt that spectacle. These were ducks unmolested, in nearly unmolested habitat—at times my 12-gauge might have dropped a dozen at a shot. These were ducks as they must have appeared in North America in the days there are no old-timers left to remember for us.

No, I will not tell you where, brother hunter. Show me your ornithologist's credentials, and take me along, and I'll show you when we get there. Not that it's all that secret. Some Uruguayans know, and once there begins to be manufacture of cheap shotguns. . . .

"Two Spaniards came," Aroldo had told me. "With a truck of ammunition, and a worker to build the hiding house, and little false ducks to swim in front of them. Ah, for three days they shot, and killed six hundred and fourteen ducks. They had a man to count, Spaniards from the Embassy."

"What happened to the ducks?" I asked.

Aroldo shrugged. Reuben, who is a sensitive man, looked sad.

Anybody here think of a way we might export some conservation practices to countries like my friend Reuben's? I like Reuben—I like Aroldo, too, but I wish there were a warden to watch him; I like Reuben's son, who is a fine natural outdoorsman, like his father. Manufacture of cheap shotguns . . . couldn't we have an alliance *against* some kinds of progress?

5:03 In this remnant of perfect habitat, the sky is empty. It is five minutes till sunset, but it is dusk already, when my last snipe does go up. I hear him before I see him. I crouch down, close to the ground, trying to expand the area of light against which he will show up, and he appears now, winging for the upper sky; but I cannot decide to shoot, shouldering my gun in that awkward position. And in another second it is too late, really too late, and I feel as if the last hunter in the world has let the last snipe go without a try.

I straighten up reluctantly, unload my gun, and wonder where I am. Suddenly I am tired, melancholy, and very hungry. I know about which way to go, and start along, calling Moon, only half lost, dragging a little. The hunting is over and home an hour away.

I think of quail hunting in Louisiana, when we crouched, straining for shots at the final covey, as I did just now for the final snipe.

I hear a roosting pheasant call.

There is a place a century away in time, called Koehler Prairie, sixty or eighty acres of this Iowa land that was never plowed or grazed. Prairie grasses still grow there, prairie flowers bloom, as they did when the buffalo passed back and forth and the Indians after them. Koehler Prairie is a park, and will be preserved.

I heard the pheasants call, hunting there one evening, not long before dark, with a group of men and three dogs spread out in front of us. It moved me a good deal, I think it moved us all; it is the sort of place where there is so much evocation that personalities are absorbed and muted in one's consciousness of history and time past. Were they pheasants coming into roost or creatures long extinct, heath hens? Were we the men we were (me, Culross, Ben, and the Commissioner), or were we plainsmen?

There are two or three such prairie preserves out here; see one when you come through Iowa. You hardly need a gun—they are rare places, where it is almost better to be a fantasist than a hunter.

I find a little road I recognize, start on it the wrong way, correct myself and turn back along it. A touch of late sun shows now, through a rift, enough to cast a pale shadow in front of me—man with gun—on the sand road.

We were on an evening march, in some loose company formation, outside of training camp. We were boys. I watched our shadows along the tall clay bank at the side of the road. We were too tired to talk, even garrulous Bobby Hirt, who went AWOL later and spent two years, so we heard, in military prison. He was a boy. We all were. But the helmeted shadows, with packs and guns in silhouette, were the shadows of soldiers—faceless, menacing, expendable. No one shadow different from the others. I could not tell you, for after training we dispersed, going out as infantry replacements, which of those boys, whose misery and defiance and occasional good times I shared for seventeen unforgotten weeks, actually were expended. Several, of course, since statistics show what they do of infantry replacements. Statistics are the representation of shadows by numbers.

My shadow on the sand road is of a different kind. I have come a little way in nineteen years, whatever the world has done. I am alone, in a solitary place, as I wish to be, accountable only as I am willing to be held so, therefore no man's statistic. Melancholy for the moment, but only because I am weary, and coming to the end of this day which, full of remembering, will be itself remembered.

Moon is beside me, tired now too, throwing his own pale dog-shadow ahead. And the hunter-shadow with him, the pheasant hanging from the hunter's belt, snipe bulging in the jacket—the image teases me. It is not the soldiers, but some other memory. An image, failing because the sun is failing, the rift closing very slowly. An image of. A hunter like. A dream? Not a dream, but the ghost of a dream, my old, hunter-and-his-dog-at-dusk dream. And the sun goes down, and the ghost with it, and the car is in sight which will carry us home.

5. The Unnatural Enemy

I DON'T SEE HOW THERE COULD BE ANY SUCH THING as a purist in crow hunting. It is not a division of gun sports with traditional customs, like those, indistinctly inherited from England, that prevent a good many North Americans from shooting sitting ducks or running pheasants, and a great many others from admitting it when they do. I assume that in England, where these traditions seem to have been formed in order to distinguish the gentlemen, who hunted for sport, from the louts, who poached out of unfashionable, lower-class hunger, crows, like other predators, were left to gamekeepers to control. In our country, even among hunters on the East Coast, where class lines have been most strongly established, gentlemanly hunting codes aren't very rigid now. The matter of conduct in the field—whether to hold oneself as sportsman, pothunter, or scourge—is one of those fuzzy things left to shift around in individual consciences and tastes. As we compete, equally and fervently, sometimes bitterly, for what game there is, every man is alternately gentleman and poacher, and every man is his own gamekeeper.

[135]

My particular taste or conscience in the gamekeeper role is not very permissive. Nothing could move me to shoot a hawk or owl, even one of the kinds that are unprotected here in Iowa—the Cooper's and sharp-shinned hawks, and the great horned owl; I admire them too much. Unlike most people I have hunted with, I do not shoot feral cats when I come upon them in quail or pheasant fields, nor permit my dogs to kill them. It is surprising, by the way, what numbers of these cats there are, all over the country—not wildcats but cats gone wild, a little tougher and better muscled than house cats but the same breed, gone back to hunting for themselves. They are charged by the Audubon Society with killing several hundred song and game birds a year per animal. Perhaps I would shoot a fox, a very high-scoring competitor for pheasants, but I do not seem to feel strongly enough about it ever to have set out after one. I am, in fact, almost exclusively guided by the precept, more particularly a conservationist's than a sportsman's, of killing creatures only in such kinds and quantities as I intend to eat.

Crows are the one exception to this, and I will have to be indulged in some free-style speculation to explain why. I admire crows, but it is a different kind of admiration from that in which I hold hawks and owls. In the latter, the raptors, it is their speed and seeming recklessness, their enormous and aloof skill as hunters, that excite me. The crow, a slow flier, uses different tools—intelligence, co-operativeness with other crows. On the one hand, there is instinct and madness (according to the falconer I know, hawks are not wise, and the one owl he tried to train was painfully stupid) that will subdue creatures several times the raptor's size; on the other hand, there is a kind of humanoid common sense that leads crows to choose such easy, if not totally defenseless, prey as eggs, carrion, and infant birds. I conclude from this that my urge to shoot crows is fundamentally a piece of anthropomorphic sentimentality, and a pretty silly one. I seem to think of owls and hawks, and even cats and foxes, as real hunters, and of crows, along with jays and magpies, as being like men who hunt from cars, jack-lighting deer at night or shooting out the window into grounded coveys of quail by day.

If this analogizing is the underlying reason for my crow hunting, the surface reasons may be a little sounder. Crows are wily enough birds to be extremely interesting to hunt. Like any bird in flight, they are hard to hit. And, because they do so much damage to other birds, particularly in areas where ducks nest, it is always open season on them, so that one may hunt them at times when no other live target is permitted.

The technique of crow hunting is complex and demanding. I would say that a friend of mine, whom I shall call Herb Mills, and I made one crow hunter between us. Herb is the man with whom I learned what little I know of the pursuit. He is, moreover, the only hunting companion with whom I have ever been completely at ease in the field; this account of our one great, successful crow hunt should demonstrate why.

Herb is a surgeon, and a lover of birds. He is a slight, deceptively relaxed-looking individual, with a mumpish face, thin brown hair, and blue eyes—beloved by children, trusted by the wives of male associates, and a positive inspiration to dogs. There are people who manage to be consistently gentle and courteous without its ever occurring to others to construe these qualities as indicating lack of force. Herb is one of them, and you would not have to know him long to realize that the force is there, all right, but most of it is directed inward to produce the tension necessary to a man who is compelled to heal. It was, then, fine but beside the point that when we hunted together Herb shot well and knew the game; much closer to the point was the fact that he had the kind of enthusiasm that made the hours outdoors worthwhile to him whether we bagged anything or not. What really counted for me was the simple pleasure of taking him away from the intensities of his calling, of seeing him released from the harassment and anxiety of dedication.

Ducks were what Herb liked best—not merely to hunt in the fall but to watch in the spring, and to read long, technical books about in winter. This was why he shared my particular malice toward crows. According to a conservation organization called Ducks Unlimited, the average adult crow destroys a hundred and twenty ducklings and duck eggs a year in the breeding areas, and our part of Iowa is a breeding area, if a marginal one. All during one fall, when I could get Herb away from the operating room and into a duckblind perhaps one morning a week, he carried a crow call. We didn't shoot crows from the blind, but often, as we walked back, we'd stop under a tree on a bank of the Iowa river and Herb would call a few times. And sometimes a crow would come.

This first bird to arrive is a kind of scout, or so we had each been told; it is quite necessary that he be shot. Otherwise, so crow hunter's belief goes, he will return and somehow advise the rest of the flock that the call he investigated was a fake. He comes gliding over, high and silent, from some unpredictable quadrant, and the need for the hunter to be concealed until he is in view usually means that there is no clear lane of fire between the hiding place and the line of his glide. Often, that fall, one or the other of us could have been seen scrambling out from under the selected tree and onto the riverbank to take an awkward, futile shot at a disappearing crow. It would have been more efficient, I concede, if we'd been willing to combine our fire, but neither Herb nor I hunts that way; it is common enough these days, and the argument runs that with game so scarce one should take as little chance as possible of losing it. But to us, a man's turn to shoot was a matter of high personal privilege. I feel the same gratitude to those who shoot at birds simultaneously with me as I have for unsolicited help at cards or crossword puzzles, if in much greater degree. Herb felt the same way, but perhaps not quite so crossly.

This being so, we missed a lot of scouting crows that fall. We dropped some, too, but only once was this followed, as it was alleged it would be, by the coming of more crows in response to renewed calling. The one time it happened, we had already stopped calling and given them up and were on our way out of hiding when they came over. Herb, whose vein of humor is a mixture of corniness and fantasy, cried, as the crows flew away untouched after our volley of late shots, that the air behind their tails was absolutely lacerated. I had other friends, severer wits, who thought Herb something of a fool for indulging in remarks like that, but I always found his stuff okay. Even when it was really clumsy (I'll try not to quote examples), it had an endearing quality for me—like the clumsiness of a hard-pulling horse, not quite used to being out of harness, trying to play a little in a pasture.

It was the following summer that I located, six miles from where I live, an enormous flock of crows. The flock was in an area of about two hundred acres of permanently flooded timber alongside the Iowa river. The water there is backed up among the trees during high water in the spring, and the land is low enough so that a lot of water stays when the river goes down. The timber is dead, water-killed, except for growths of small willows here and there, and the place has been a swamp long enough for swamp plants to have taken hold among the tree roots. Wood ducks, teal, and a few mallards and pintails nest there. Herons and egrets feed in the shallower parts, and it supports dozens of grackles, hundreds of swallows, and thousands of mosquitoes. Fields, which flood too early in the year to be of much use for agriculture, run down to the edge of the water; the government dam has taken them out of cultivation. A century ago, they were productive, and the settlers fenced them, as they often did around here, with living fences of Osage orange trees. These are small, tough trees, and make good fence rows; other, larger trees are established among them by now. The fence rows run through the fields, perpendicular to the swamp, and stop at its edge.

What I noticed, walking along to see the water birds one brilliant morning, was that crows came rather steadily out of the swamp and across the fields, following lines of flight parallel to the orange-tree fences. It may have taken a dozen separate crows flying out this way at intervals to get my attention away from the more fascinating birds, but when I had stopped and counted five crows following the same pattern in perhaps twenty minutes, I concluded that a major flock was roosting in the swamp. They must have been moving out from the roost for the day's feeding in cultivated fields. I felt a little lame in making such an easy observation, for I'd come to know that swamp pretty well, yet so common is it in the Midwest for there to be a crow somewhere in the landscape that I had taken no particular notice of these before.

My children treat decoy birds as casual playthings, leaving them around almost anywhere, and one had left a horned-owl decoy in my car that day. I walked back and got it, and carried it along to the edge of the swamp. It was made with a hole in the bottom so that one could place it on a pole or limb. I saw a sapling standing out about fifty feet from one of the fence rows, went to it, bent it down, and set my decoy on its top, where it fitted rather loosely; I let the sapling spring back up again, and there was an owl, sitting in a tree. Such decoys are used in crow hunting because the great horned owl is almost the only serious natural enemy crows have. (I cannot count man's enmity for any animal as natural.)

I went back to the fence and sat under an orange tree, watching the decoy to see whether a passing crow might attack it. I suppose I waited nearly an hour in hiding, but I didn't mind; the morning had turned hot, and I enjoyed the rest. A red-shouldered hawk was the only bird that come over my decoy, drifting slowly overhead, wheeling suddenly when it saw the supposed owl and dropping to smash at it so quickly that the thing was off the tree and lying on the ground before I quite realized what was happening. I had seen many crows out over the fields as I waited, however, and by the time I was ready to go home for lunch I knew what part of the swamp the crows came from. As soon as I got home, I called Herb's house.

Herb's wife, Mardu, said that he had just finished lunch, though he hadn't eaten much. He was exhausted; one of those marathon operations . . . just pushed his food away . . . damn good lunch—soufflé. He was lying down now, she said, and she'd rather not call him to the phone, if I didn't mind. She said she'd already put her foot down on his returning to the hospital to lead his dippy little flock of medical students around the post-operative ward. I was by then looking for nothing more than a pause in which to say that I'd call back later, when Herb, having apparently heard my name, picked up the bedroom extension phone and said hello.

I said that I'd located a concentration of crows and hoped

we could go after them sometime.

"I think we should, sometime," Herb said. "I think we ought to do that in about ten or fifteen minutes."

Mardu Mills didn't exactly scream, but I think it was only because she had a child napping. It took a while for them to work through her protests and his counters, but eventually he finished denying the heat of the day, his own tiredness, and the possibility that he was crazy, and Mardu hung up, leaving us free to talk.

Then we indulged in a piece of foolishness that was mine, not his. I always seem to want to say everything that is in my mind about an episode of hunting or fishing, proposed or just past, over the telephone, even though I may be talking with someone I will be seeing almost immediately. I said we'd better take along insect repellent. I said I had just bought a new crow call. Herb said he had a new reed for his. Herb said he was going to shoot No. 5 shells. I said that this year's hatch of crows should be big enough to fly with the flock by now. Herb said the teal might be nesting for a second time, hatching a second brood. I said the wind might come up and cool things off. Herb said he'd read a new report on crows in Canada—between one September and the next August they had destroyed three and a half million ducklings and duck eggs. I think I even repeated the one about each adult crow's getting a hundred and twenty ducklings and eggs, which Herb had undoubtedly told me in the first place. I was too excited to stop talking. If things worked as I felt they would, this would be our first productive crow hunt, and, for that matter, a real hunt of any kind was exciting so far out of normal shooting season. I have an almost total apathy toward shooting birds of clay.

I was ready when Herb arrived. My own wife had had her turn at mentioning what going out in the noonday sun might indicate about our mental health, my children were persuaded this was not a summer outing they'd enjoy, and the new patches were dry on my hip boots. Herb noticed I was wearing the boots and said, "It was kind of you not to mention water toys. Now you'll have to do all the splashing," and we both laughed as if he'd said something much funnier. I was absurdly happy by then. I felt as I had the one time a friend and I played hooky from our small-city high school, not to see an afternoon movie or sit near a jukebox but to go fishing. Now, as then, it seemed so much more gratifying to fit the physical world than to try to control it or let it be manipulated for us, as it would be if Herb was kept comfortable in an air-conditioned hospital with his cases, or I in an air-conditioned study with my books. To have our shotguns out in August, with the oil liquefying on the barrels, to be wearing hunting jackets with the lovely weight of shells in the pockets, to be heading where live birds flew in such a season seemed illegally fine—contrary, if not to the laws of the Conservation Commission, then to the dreary laws of adult life. It was important, from this standpoint, that it should have been a weekday afternoon.

Back we drove to the swamp, parked the car nearby, and started along the edge, stopping to smear our faces first with insect repellent, then with mud to cut the glare skin makes. By the time we had walked a quarter of a mile in the blissful, sweltering miasma of swamp air, the sweat streaks through the mud coating on Herb's face and the white left around his eyes had made him so ridiculous that I couldn't look at him without laughing, and, from his reactions, I don't suppose that I looked any better.

At the edge of the swamp, just under what I calculated to be the principal flyway, we fixed a place to hide. We piled up a row of brush, starting a few feet out from the trunk of a big, half-dead oak and curving it back and around in the shape of a horseshoe, with the open end pointing towards the tree. We cut bundles of swamp grass to cover the horseshoe and piled them up until the whole thing began to look like a large, untidy bird's nest. I had two crow decoys now, and I set them in it while Herb's back was turned, so that their glass eyes peered at him over the edge. "Your eggs done hatched, Mr. Interlocutor," I said. There were enough live branches on the tree to give us cover from the top, but the ones that projected over the swamp were leafless, leaving the field of fire reasonably clear.

"Let's put these children to work in the show, Mr. Bones," Herb said firmly, taking up the crow decoys. We

WINTER GEAR

placed one on a patch of bare ground in the field behind the blind, set up on a two-foot stick so that it appeared to be gazing into the swamp, and the other off to the right on a bare limb that projected out over the water. When we got started, live crows were supposed to take these as the source of our calling.

Then I took the owl decoy, fastened my boot tops to my belt, waded into the slack, deceptive water in front of our shooting place, and thought for a moment I might never stop sinking. For a man who chooses to spend as much time in mud as I do, I have more than an ordinary fear of it. Once, in Uruguay, I saw a giant hare leap into quicksand and disappear; he went under as fast as a stick does tossed into a sinkhole in one of our marshes here. Always when I am snipe hunting, I skirt the softer-looking places. I mention this because the mood of the day was such that it hardly occurred to me to be frightened when my right knee went out of sight.

[143]

An instant later, I stopped sinking and I was able to struggle forward onto slightly firmer mud. There were numbers of small dead trees sticking out at odd, wind-tipped angles from the shallow water, and it was easy enough to find one lying on its side and twist free what roots were left. This made a pole, about eighteen feet long, to set the owl on. I raised it upright and carried it, a step at a time, to the center of the open-water area. Then I set the base carefully into the water, pressed down hard when I felt it reach mud, and found too late that I had picked another soft spot. The thing went down four feet with my weight on it, pitching me forward into the puddle. I got a good mouthful of swampwater, and mud in my hair and eyes, and before I could recover, Herb was floundering toward me, bootless. I raised up to my knees, laughing at him, and told him to get back.

"Hell," he said, reaching me anyway. "It's nice in here."

When we had finished straightening the owl around, I was wet to the shoulders and Herb to the waist, but we didn't mind; we were seldom altogether dry when we hunted.

We sloshed back to the bank, where the guns were lying. I wiped my hands on grass and picked mine up. "There's no sense both crowding into the blind," I said. "I think I'll go back across," and I pointed to a brushy mud flat that formed the opposite edge of this first of the many shallow pools that marked the low points in the swamp. Fortunately, I had left my jacket with my gun when I waded out to place the owl, so my shells were still dry. I rolled the jacket up to carry under my arm, took up the gun in my other hand, and went off, boot by boot, through the same puddle of stagnant water, to where the roots of a huge old tree, lying on its side on the mud flat, formed a shallow cave, with thin screens of willows on either side. Leaning back into the cave, feeling light and free because here the mud clung up only as far as my ankles, I put the jacket on, loaded the gun, found my crow call, and waved to Herb that I was ready. I could see him through the willows, but not very clearly. We had noticed no crows in the air while setting up, and that was very hopeful. When crows see men go into hiding, they are smart enough to avoid those places for a long while—even, some say, until they count the same number of men (up to three) go out again as have gone in.

As soon as I waved, Herb began blowing his call. I held mine, a five-inch wooden instrument flared at one end and with a mouthpiece at the other, listening to him. Four caws, fairly rapid, pitched high, and each descending slightly into a second partial syllable, formed the attraction call, or highball, according to the printed instructions that came with my instrument, and this was what Herb was blowing. It duplicates the alarm raised by a cruising crow when it happens upon an owl and begins calling up others for the chase. I listened as Herb blew three series, and then, when he was two caws into a fourth, joined in, imagining myself a second crow attracted by the first and just discovering what the trouble was.

"Caa-aaw, caa-aaw—" Almost immediately there was a crow floating over us, looking down.

It took me completely by surprise and must have startled Herb, too, for it came out of the field behind him. I think it must have been a bird that happened to be on its way to the roost when our calling started, a bird that swung over from a line of flight already established rather than one attracted from much distance. If our belief in the need to kill the first crow was correct, then it was a good thing Herb was a fast shot. While I was still gawking, his Winchester pump gun fired just once, and the crow tumbled wing over wing down through the air and into the water at my left, giving some rather distressing caws of its own. For a moment, it seemed almost to sit and float like a water bird, trying to compose itself, as spent shot from Herb's shell pattered into the water around it.

There is another piece of crow-hunting lore or technique we might have followed. This suggests that wounded crows should be left alive, even caught and put in a sack, so that their cries of pain will add authenticity to the sounds of battle. This is said to be very effective at bringing others, but I had no will to test it. Nor was there any need for me to ask Herb how he might feel. He couldn't see the downed bird from where he was, and about the time he called to ask if I knew where it had landed, I shot the crow, and it floated off dead, moving with the impact of the pellets until it came to rest on a small extrusion of mud.

It was hard to believe, as we began the attraction call again, that the sound of two shots wouldn't keep other crows away forever, yet all authorities and our own meagre experience insisted that one of the basics of crow hunting is to keep shooting and calling simultaneously. There is, in fact, a piece of equipment offered in the Abercrombie & Fitch catalogue that provides ultimate simultaneity—a portable, transistorized phonograph on which a field recording of live crows calling may be played at great volume. It costs a hundred and twenty-five dollars, and I wonder where it is that they hunt crows so hard as to justify the expense. The machines, it is my impression, were originally made for duck hunters, and I guess they must have worked all too well, since the use of duck recordings is now outlawed. They're probably extraordinary on crows. I might like to try one; I can't be sure.

I can be quite sure that Herb and I produced no such volume or authenticity with our wooden crow calls, yet we had hardly started blowing again before crows began to answer us from the interior of the swamp, first two or three together, then what sounded like a dozen of them. We called for perhaps ten minutes, and the answers seemed to shift from place to place at first, then grew gradually more concerted and closer. The real birds' voices seemed barbarous and angry as they approached, and I heard Herb increase the tempo of his calling, lowering the pitch enough to get a snarl into it. He had shifted, he told me later, to the fighting call. That seemed to do it, for just as I was starting to change position slightly, trying to get a boot loose from the mud, a black shape came sailing low out of the brush beside me, saw Herb, flared, and started back. I couldn't move that boot. All I could do was lean back and swing my gun straight up till it pointed right over where my head had been; by the time I was on the bird and willing to shoot, I was pretty well doubled backward. It may have been the most difficult shot I've ever made in my life, for the bird actually fell directly behind me, about fifteen feet back onto the trunk of the same tree whose roots I was standing in. I had to get the boot loose, turn, and take two steps sideways to see it. Herb said afterward that he was awed by the shot, and I confess I felt a little the same way myself.

"Here they come!" he yelled as I was still peering back and congratulating myself, and I struggled into position in time to see five or six crows between us and the sky, flying through in different directions, at different velocities and different heights. I emptied my gun wildly at them, and missed all five shots while Herb hit two. Chastened and a little confused, I resumed calling, forgetting to reload. Fortunately, Herb remembered, for when two more came he was ready and he shot a double on them, two clean kills—his turn to be impressive.

The swamp behind me was full of cawing by now, and Herb and I added all we could to it. I told myself to calm down, got loaded, got my feet arranged comfortably and my gun and body hidden again. I saw a crow flit through a space between two trees. I saw another bolting across the sky over-

COORDINATED CALLING AND SHOOTING

head, high and out of range. They then began to come in, diving at the owl singly and in pairs, and we shot and hit, shot and missed, called and waded, in a growing ecstasy. I was out of my cave now, needing a wider field of fire, and the mud was up to my knees, so that I could turn only from the waist to shoot. A crow came from the right, and I got him, but couldn't recover in time to shoot at another overhead. I went forward onto my knees in the water to correct this, freeing myself and having more surface under me against the mud. I was in water to the waist now, and my boots were full, but I could swivel, turn, and wriggle pretty freely. I'd transferred my shells into the two breast pockets of my shirt to keep them dry, and the heavy bulges interfered a little with the swinging of my gun, but it hardly bothered me. Sweat running into my eyes didn't bother me, nor did clouds of mosquitoes buzzing around, some getting through the repellent now, nor did the smell of stagnant water choking my nose and throat, nor even the call clenched in my teeth, through which I gasped, keeping my hands free for the gun. In the success and absurdity of the afternoon, each of these discomforts became a wild little contribution to happiness. I dropped another crow, and another. I was a mechanism designed to withstand swamps and destroy crows. Three came, and I hit one, saw the other two wheel toward Herb, and saw him get them both, and I spat out my call to yell in exuberance. Then came another, and I shot him twice, killing him with the first shot and almost disintegrating him with the second, which took him as he fell.

There was a lull. I got my call back, wiped my hands, and reloaded. My mouth ached, but I don't know if it was from grinning or grasping the crow call, and I was tired of being wet. I got up, moved back towards my tree, and hoisted myself astraddle of a big projecting root. There were bodies of crows all around and on the water, and I saw movement in one and shot it. A single crow went over, much too high to shoot at, and Herb produced a new sound on his crow call, a sad, descending caw, which the high crow echoed, and I guessed what it was from having seen such a call named in the instruction book—the sorrow call.

A moment after, there came a chorus like nothing I have

heard before or since, a chorus of furious and concerted calls —the whole flock, it had to be, flying towards us now from their roost to defend their swamp. I did not take the crow call from my pocket. My hunting intuitions are reasonably good, and a strong one now suggested that there'd be no need for further calling. Crazily, it occurred to me I might just as well shoot down our owl decoy, for it was no longer that that they were attacking. I felt that the foolish, infuriated birds must know quite well now who and what we were, and that they would come attacking us. I could hear wings in the air, and a second later it was full of crows—twenty or thirty I could see and many more I couldn't.

One flew at me, or so I think, and, feeling the grin on my face again, I killed him. Herb was firing, too, but not at the five that swept toward me from the right. I got one of those and missed a second. Then I swung after the one I'd missed and got him with a long, long shot I had no right to make. And then another, snap-shooting to the opposite side as he climbed, and then I had no shells for the half dozen that came retreating from Herb's direction. They were routed, they were gone. We could hear them call, mutter, and mourn, back now in the interior.

"I got four of those," I yelled at Herb, and he held up three fingers and shouted that he must look for a cripple. Setting my gun in the fork of a smaller root, I got up into standing position on the large root I'd been straddling. I looked back into the swamp now, from the slight height, in the direction of the crows' retreat. I couldn't hear them any longer, nor were there any cripples, but I did see something quite unexpected—the remains of a road. It went straight back through the swamp; the rocks and gravel that had been its bed were slightly exposed in places, making easy walking to the inside. It must, I thought, go to the roost or very near it. One small pool to cross, no worse than the one I'd crossed already, and I'd be on my way. As for Herb, he was muddy enough not to mind more wading.

Yet when I looked at the next pool, I was reluctant to step into it, and it seemed my fear of mud was back. I turned and looked across for Herb. For a moment I couldn't locate him;

then he waved, and I saw that he had climbed a little way up into a tree. "Looking at the road?" he called, and I felt obscurely apprehensive at the knowledge that he had seen it, too. I watched him slip down from the tree, walk along the bank, shoot the cripple he had located, then return to where he'd been shooting from, and sit down. I found myself nodding at him, feeling relieved. I got back into the mud, picking up my gun and retrieving my owl on the way to join him.

Herb gave me a dry cigarette. Then he said, "What were we going to do, after that last grand sortie they made? Jump on our damn chargers, swim the moat, and storm their castle?"

"I know," I said, but it has taken a certain amount of afterthought to determine what it was I knew. Often in our prematurely grey republic we must make up our rules even as we act upon them, and sometimes the action has actually preceded the rules, perhaps by quite a long while. Had I been alone out there in the swamp, for example, I would not have gone on to shoot more crows at the roost, which would probably have driven the flock away from the swamp for good, and it might have taken a long time for me to decide that my failure to do so was anything other than quitting. Had I been hunting with my friend X or my friend Y, either one would have insisted that we go. X is a real exterminator when he gets going, and his rule is "Get every one you can. That's what you came out for, isn't it?" As for Y, he'd have taken the duty to control predators quite grimly, acting not so much in accordance with a rule as with whole books of rules, of the kind that proliferate any time one mistakes a rationalization for a moral imperative. We'd have had to be seriously pure knights, consecrated avengers of the innocent duck, in order to go on to the roost for more shooting. And whatever the anthropomorphic bent of my mind, it is not so complete that I ever took myself for anything but a hunter having a hunt—a predator countless centuries removed from his motive, deserving therefore a lower place on any evolutionary scale of predators than crows themselves, or shrike or even magpies.

Demonic X and Implacable Y, I'll take Herb's kind of rule. Herb, whom we all three knew, was a comforter by nature. His rules—like all good rules, as far as I'm concerned

[150]

—were a comfort. X, the crows are still out there in the marsh each year, and I've been out to hunt them again, and I shall neither take you nor tell you where they are. Y, what a man does for enjoyment ought to end when the pleasure runs out. "Let him alone," says the barroom fighter of the man he's downed. "I've had my fun."

It was Y, by the way, who complained to X and me once about Herb's penchant for inverting proverbs, but I still like the comfortable rule he made for us by inverting one as we walked back to the car that day. "Kill and let kill," he said, smiling. "How's that?"

Herb Mills' practice took him away from here a year ago to new tensions and responsibilities in a distant place, but I hope there is someone there who gets him out from time to time to hunt. If there is, I envy him. For myself, I go crow shooting several times a year—by myself, generally, unless my wife or one of the children cares to come along. And that completes the gamekeeping report, except for one note.

As we drove away from the swamp, I said to Herb, "We've never hunted upland game together. When you do, do you shoot those wretched hunting cats?"

I knew what his answer had to be, of course. It was only that I wanted to hear him say, with his usual courtesy, that he never had.

6. Warm Again

MAY ONE WRITE ABOUT HUNTING AND NOT WRITE about deaths? The deaths inflicted, the death that one will die? It seems as impermissible to avoid as it is impossible to render.

For several weeks now, ever since pheasant season ended, I have come to my study daily to begin setting down coherently a hunter's view of death. It is to be illustrated with tales and anecdotes, drawn from documents and recollections; I have several beginnings, and some middle paragraphs, and an ending. But they do not cohere.

It seems probable to me that I have no view of death, only feelings. That I know a good deal about death, without finding anything in it that bears thinking on. That I can offer no well-structured composition, then; only the materials from which I have failed to compose it, if they are of any interest. These are: remembered conversations, a few lines from letters, a number of notes, one of the false beginnings, some items from an income-tax return, and a passage of narrative. They will be dated approximately, capriciously arranged; and if you care to read them, you will know what I know of that matter and how I feel.

August 1961, excerpt from a business letter from New York.
"I enjoyed meeting your friend Henry Akers, and it seems possible we will come to terms. I hope so. He told me, by the way, the story of how he saved your life while duck hunting . . ."
He did? Henry? I hadn't thought of it that way. I am very reluctant to think that my life was ever saved by anything except unmerited good luck and a strong predisposition not to risk it. I don't mean to say that Henry wasn't helpful on the morning he's referring to, of course he was . . .
Henry, old friend, shall we compare versions of this thing?
We were hunting on our Iowa river sandbank with Leo Ferguson, the student who spent that cold winter with his wife and baby in an off-square shack, a so-called summer cottage by the river. We would leave whichever car we were driving by the Ferguson's unpainted door, between five and six each morning, and walk down through the woods; then along the river bank where it dropped steeply away from a soybean field, through woods again and out onto the sand in the dark, by the dark river, a quarter mile below Leo's. Sometimes, if the headlights woke him, Leo'd go with us. Among the clumps of willow growing on the sandbank we'd find the burlap sack we'd hidden when we left the day before, with ten mallard decoys in it, and wade into the shallow water in front of us, careful not to go out too far, for the bottom dropped away under one's feet where the main current ran.
That morning Leo was along. It was the first or second of December, and there'd been a week of quite cold weather. The still, shallow water where we put the decoys was covered with thin ice and there were thicker chunks bobbing past in the river itself. You and I had hip boots on—Leo didn't. So you and I placed the decoys, not too carefully—stringing them out parallel with the edge of the bank, with a few bunched up at the center of the string; they were inexpensive fibre decoys,

[153]

Carrylites I think. While we were wading around, breaking up the thin ice and floating the jagged sheets out towards the current with our toes, a pair of ducks came by, low and whistling, just over our heads, and Leo said, when we came out:

"I could have got two ducks and two hunters with a single shot if I'd been alert."

Actually, it was still a minute or two before legal shooting time, and we argued whether or not they could have been shovelers—it seemed to me rather late and rather cold for shovelers still to be around, but you insisted.

We got into the willows, then, Leo downstream on the left, you in the center, me upstream on the right—about fifteen-yard intervals, was it? The intervals were established by where the willows clumped thickly enough to make good hiding. They were bare of foliage by then, and we'd been carrying in extra brush and grass all week and weaving it among the little trunks.

There was nothing stirring that morning early, though as always we'd been hopeful driving down, speaking of how cold weather and wind might have the ducks moving; duck hunters, like skiers, watch the thermometer with perverse eyes, comforted only when the temperature drops.

But the wind went down as the sun came up that morning, the sky was clear and brilliant blue, and the big chunks of ice out in the river gleamed so brightly that my eyes smarted. Where did the ducks come from finally? I don't remember—from up river, I think, a little bunch of seven or eight mallards to which I called. I was a proved, tested, and endorsed duck caller by then, having managed to get ducks in once before, six or eight days earlier, but I was still surprised to have it work. The ducks swung towards us without losing much speed, circled over our heads and towards the decoys about forty yards up, and then saw one of us—me perhaps—and flared. They climbed straight up. I swung my gun up at the instant when they seemed to stand in the air, braking to change direction, got on a drake by chance—a fine, big green-headed drake, moved nicely with him and fired. He was probably forty-five yards out and away, and I was aware that you'd fired too. I

[154]

don't think Leo got a shot, and they were past so fast that neither you nor I shot more than once. But he fell! The drake fell. There was an instant when I didn't know—then I saw his wings fold, looking straight up my gun barrel, and he dropped through the air, turning once slowly as he fell and landing dead on his back in the water, just past where the decoys were.

We yelled simultaneously, joyfully: "I got him."

And you cried, appalled: "No, I got him."

And I, for I'd paid no attention to your shot: "I did, I got him." We were being about as inventive conversationally as characters in a serious comic strip, but perhaps you wanted that duck, at that moment, as badly as I did. We were both shouting crossly and you yielded to my indignation, made more fervent probably by my being aware that it was quite possible, the way I shot that fall, that I had missed, after all—I will never know which of us was really entitled to that bird or whether we both were.

You yelled, in some alarm: "If you got him, you'd better get him." And I became aware that the duck was slowly floating away. I ran out of my hiding place to the edge of the water, and thought to lay down the gun. I waded through the decoys, trotting and splashing, and came to water over my knees. The duck was in the current, now, just past my reach, not the main current but a slighter one that ran beside it. He was being moved downstream and slightly out towards the center of the river. I stretched my arm towards him, shuffling my feet sideways and a little outwards, and still couldn't reach.

I kept moving down parallel with his movement, and then tried a long step, towards the center of the river, and the water was around my thighs at the boot tops. I remember thinking, deciding, "Okay, I'll get water in my boots," as I shuffled downstream a little farther, and then took a real stride towards him. I got the tip of my mitten on the duck, but couldn't grasp it as the water poured in, curiously warm, heated momentarily by body heat inside the boots. I had to have the drake; we had hunted thirty mornings by then and not got a dozen ducks among us, and the two or three I'd taken home had been pretty enough but not colorful. This mallard gleamed like jade, floating away in the sunlight, and I thought, "Oh, hell, I'm wet anyway," and dived in after him, padded clothing, hunting coat and all, breasting into the icy river, getting a muddy mouthful of it, and seized the drake. Then, grasping it, smiling at an ice cake that went by, I felt for bottom with my feet and there wasn't any. I turned with the drake towards the bank, treading water, and saw how far the current had taken me.

Already I was below the sand bank, below the place where one could climb out of the river. My boots were full, my clothes immersed, and in front of me was a sheer, undercut bank of frozen mud, twenty feet high. I saw you running along the edge up there, Leo after you, and I wondered why you seemed so concerned—I had the duck, didn't I? Then as I turned downstream, still with that false feeling of warmth, for the water had not worked past all my clothing, I saw what I ought to have remembered, that this bank continued steep and undercut a quarter-mile before the next shallow place.

I must have looked entirely helpless in the current, clutching my dead duck and still, for the moment, buoyant, but I didn't feel helpless nor did it occur to me to be frightened. I did not realize that the trapped air in my boots and clothing was acting as a sort of life preserver, but that it could not stay trapped for long—I thought I was keeping myself up by the water-treading.

Forty feet below, in by the bank, was an eddy full of brush, trash, and driftwood, a place where the water whirled briefly around some sunken snag. The steep bank was a little more gradual there and there was even a narrow mud shelf a few inches above water level. I saw you sliding down the bank to the precarious shelf at about the same time I decided that was the place to swim for. I pushed the drake out in front of me and began to side-stroke towards the eddy. It seemed quite easy. The strokes gave me direction and the current gave me movement. All I had to do was steer myself, it seemed, and my main task was to keep the prize in my control, nudging it towards the bank and a little upstream at the end of each stroke so that it was never below me. Did I seem out of my head? Perhaps I was.

As I came in, just above the eddy, I got the duck balanced on my right hand and gave it a shot-putter's toss in front of me, up onto the shelf, and felt a certain distress that you didn't pick it up to admire. You were holding out a branch for me to grab instead. So I grabbed it, you hauled in on it, pulling me to the edge, and then you grabbed my arms and hauled me out at some risk of going in yourself.

"Isn't he beautiful?" I said, meaning the duck.

"You're rather beautiful yourself," you said. "Come on, we've got to wring you out."

You pushed and Leo hauled me up the bank, and I suppose you must be right. I had been in a good deal more danger than I recognized, and still was, for at that point I said I thought I'd lie down and rest; I said the swim had tired me and I was going to catch my breath and admire my duck, but you and Leo kept me on my feet and made me walk all the way back up to Leo's house.

It was a long way in those dripping clothes, many wet layers—did you drag me along at times? I remember stripping and chattering by the stove in the cabin; putting on some old clothes of Leo's and the overcoat he came to class in; feeling quite exhilarated by the huge cups of coffee Edith Ferguson got up to make for us, and trying to think how to tell her not to make another pot because it seemed to me coffee must be such an expense on a student budget.

We had to return to the sandbar for our guns while my clothes dried, and on the way up again, almost casually, I shot another duck over the soybean field. There was no trouble retrieving that one, of course, but you took the occasion to point out that the thing to have done if it, too, had fallen in the current was to walk along the bank, watching it, as far as necessary, till it floated in and caught on something.

It was a shoveler female, and you reminded me that I'd said it was impossible, saying to Leo: "No, no, Leo. Not a shoveler. It's a scaup with a deformed bill."

"A grey-billed spoon-billed bluebill," Leo agreed.

Now you remember that as the morning you saved my life.

Quite right, but quite curious. All right. I'm ready to concede. Until this letter came, I was perfectly grateful to you,

SMART RETRIEVE (II)

but on two less vital counts—that you yielded your claim to
the mallard, and that you didn't treat me as something fragile
when walking along in Leo's blue tweed overcoat, I proved so
utterly in error about shovelers.

Note, undated. That he will die is the bad news in any man's
life, and the sources from which he has it altogether reliable.
I feel for it a loathing far deeper than fear. Can it be because
I loathe it that I go out to find its counterpart when, in hunting, I kill? (That is a made-up guess, carrying no conviction.)

I have not loathed the fact of my own eventual death
steadily and always. There was a time, during the war, when
I was somewhat in love with it—I can remember that without
remembering how it felt. Anyway, it was puppy love. Infatuation. I was twenty then, and not a hunter.

Passage underlined last winter, in Walden. "The grand necessity for our bodies is to keep warm, to keep the vital heat in us.'' I underlined it because it touched an image I have, a primitive image: Death is letting something in, letting coolness into the air-tight container of Thoreau's vital heat.

Of course if the coolness be cold enough, and the container insufficiently protected, no wound need be made. But in shooting we seek to breach the container, to let the coolness inside.

A pheasant flies up, intact, incorporate; pellets enter it at a number of places, making small holes from which, in Thoreau's primitive image, warmth spills out. In mine, coolness, which has pressed around that body ceaselessly all through its existence, finds the tiny holes to let it in.

Note, today's date (December 26, 1962), on the paragraphs above, and on the ones below as well. All ideas of death are primitive. My ''letting something in'' is a simple primitive idea. A religious person's heaven, hell, and purgatory, populated with billions of survived souls, is an elaborate primitive idea.

But of course those aren't ideas; they are, respectively, a metaphor and a conceit. The mind flinches into figures of speech when we direct it to consider death. Sometimes, as I shall illustrate next, there is another kind of flinching that goes on.

A false beginning, December 23, 1962. (If I understand the term ''action painting,'' it describes an unrevisable, spontaneous way of covering canvas, calling for a good deal of physical movement on the part of the painter. This beginning, in the same way, was action writing. I did it a day or two ago, while it still seemed I could control this material, and it goes rather quickly into a description of just what was happening to me as I tried to write. I have transcribed it without change, and since I picked up a line and a notion from it for use elsewhere, you may recognize the repetitions.)

Warm Again

Finally (I wrote) one cannot think seriously of hunting without thinking seriously of death, the deaths one causes and the death that one will die. This is not a matter I, for one, can contemplate for long. This may be a matter of character: I am unable to credit the consoling if rather self-worshiping fantasy of religious persons that something of me will survive my dying. There is thus nothing further to think of death than that it is an end, there being nothing to contemplate in a state of blankness ... Here is an interesting thing: before I could type the words "an end," just above, I was taken with the need to sneeze, one of those deep, gasping irresistible tickles crawling up the throat, which made my hands come off the typewriter keys, one to cover my mouth and the other to keep my balance. I had no sooner discharged this sneeze than I felt another gathering itself. My whole upper body was involved this time and my hands useless—it nearly pitched me onto the desk top. The third in the series was there before I had recovered from the second, quick, harsh, raw, and filled my eyes with water. I got my left index finger to the *a* now, my mind still chiefly occupied with whether "an end" was the phrase I wanted—I thought I'd type it out and see—but the fourth sneeze came, a dry, painful one this time, to pull the finger back off. I began to wonder at myself; the fifth was coming, my nose was engorged, my eyes squinted, almost closed from sinus pressure; and I thought—what the hell? Am I so totally outraged at recalling that I must die that I go into convulsions rather than bring it up? A sixth, almost diffident sneeze, a shame-faced sneeze—caught red-throated, sneezing off a topic—rather like the answer, and I thought: All right. Finger to the *a* or sneeze your life away avoiding it. A mild, sneaking-away, sorry, can't-help-it kind of tickle—I typed "an end," I typed a comma—and the seventh sneeze, the final one, hardly even convulsive, came out like a cough, and I was able to go on.

(So I went on. I typed the clause which follows "an end"; then it occurred to me to write out the description of the sneezing. I found, about the time I finished, that I seemed to have to urinate—something I'd taken care of not long before, and forbade it. I commanded myself to type on, another page or two, and did—and they are as dull a couple of pages of prose as I think I've ever written. They go beyond dullness—or did;

they are safely thrown away—they were witless, morbid, weakly whimsical. Rereading them I couldn't help speculating that, having failed to defeat me with sallies at the throat and at the bladder, the defense had grown subtler and afflicted my mind. And so I resolved on the strategy in which you find me engaged: to fragment my attack in the hope that by hitting out wild, striking different blows from different directions, I can manage to penetrate the surface of the subject somewhere.)

From a letter to Herb Mills, December 1, 1962
"This pheasant season I have had the same curious thing happen three times, curious because it never happened in any pheasant season past. The first time I was with a man who had not hunted before. We were walking on each edge of a long, rectangular stand of smartweed, with Moon going back and forth through the weeds between us. As we came near the end, I shouted that my friend had better be ready; I was fairly certain there'd been a bird running ahead of the dog, and that when he reached the fringe of the cover he'd fly, which was just what happened. The bird flew left, towards Dick and I waited for him to shoot; it was his first shot ever and after a moment it was apparent that he wasn't going to get it off— safety trouble or something. So I fired myself, a little late, and then he did too; it was as if my gun had touched his off; and then we laughed and cursed for it seemed we'd both missed. I watched the bird—it was the only cock we'd seen in a long afternoon of flushing hens—fly off, across a road and out over an uncut hayfield. I was watching for him to set his wings and glide, thinking I might be able to mark him down if he didn't go too far; he was then about a hundred yards away. Suddenly, instead of gliding downward as they do, he began to stroke very strongly and to rise, higher than I ever saw a pheasant fly before. He got fifty or sixty yards into the air, higher than the tops of the walnut trees next to the hayfield, and then seemed to fail; fought his wings and fell, whirling slowly down like a leaf.

"It didn't make an sense to me. I thought perhaps one of us had got a random pellet in a wing, and that the pellet had worked itself in somehow until the bird was abruptly unable to fly. Dick and I ran across the road; I was explaining that I thought we must have a cripple over there, a runner, and that our best chance of finding him was to get the dog trailing as quickly as possible. To the right of where I thought the cock had fallen, growing under the walnut trees, was a stand of giant horseweed, taller than my head, and thick; I thought surely the bird would have run into it, and called Moon over there immediately. When he didn't seem to pick up any scent after ten or fifteen minutes, we let him cast around the hayfield for another ten or fifteen; no luck. Not a sign.

"Perhaps you already know the solution but I didn't until a week later. I was hunting south of town, had another high rise out of high cover, and shot the cock from underneath as he sailed over my head. A few feathers floated down, but the bird kept going. He went seventy or eighty yards, made that fight for altitude, and fell. This time I was really discouraged, but at least he'd fallen on somewhat barer ground, in a closely grazed pasture. Perhaps I could at least find something— feathers, a drop of blood—at the place he landed. I went there directly, having marked it pretty well, and there was the bird, lying dead. He hadn't moved. Neither, I decided sadly, had the first, not even enough to make scent for the dog. Neither did the third, for the same strange thing happened a week later.

"I examined the second and third birds when I dressed them. One had a pellet in his brain, the other one in his heart."

(I think I know what Herb will say, if he has time to answer. I think he will say that the quick clean kill is accomplished by shock—by riddling the bird with many pellets, or shooting something with more impact, a much larger shot-size than the number sixes that I use. The clean wound in a vital spot kills rather slowly.)

Something Henry Akers once said, four or five years ago.
"You can shoot a man right through the heart with a .22 bullet and not stop him. He could still live long enough to chase you with a knife and kill you before he died. You'd want something

like a .45, that hits like a fist. That's why I'd rather use a shotgun, hunting squirrels. I've shot too many .22 bullets right through a squirrel's body, and seen him run along a limb afterwards, and dive into a hole in the tree. Hit him with a shotgun, he drops."

Note, on yellowed paper, more than ten years old. Guns are garbage. The army left me feeling tired and contemptuous of guns and shooting. I saw too many creeps and idiots in those four years who could handle, dismantle, reassemble, and shoot guns well. I did have a certain dilettante admiration for the madman ingenuity that went into the designing of the Browning Automatic Rifle, one of which I carried for a time; it took one of us more earnest creeps, a slightly advanced idiot, to comprehend the B.A.R. On single shots, once I learned the trigger, I shot it better than I did a rifle. But there was something archaic about the B.A.R., as there was about the water-cooled machine guns—they were First World War weapons. There was a kind of elegance about the B.A.R., a fineness in the making. Style. The cheap little grease guns with their crude, stamped metal look, which seemed to be replacing B.A.R.'s in the Pacific, were dreary to look at and hold, though, I suppose, more murderous. The bazooka, which was the only rocket weapon we saw, and a prototype, I suppose, of what infantry arms are becoming, was, of course, extraordinarily powerful and perfectly stupid-looking. War was coming into the twentieth century, all right, a crude, vicious century in which there is nothing less stylish than to be a soldier. Like so much we have now, the weapons are drab to look at, routinely effective, and made for morons to operate, like television sets and washing machines—squads of moronic engineers labor together designing all the superduper into them; thus the weapon's power having been built in at the factory, it does not depend on any sort of talent in the operator. The control of a swordsman meant a good deal more than the temper of his weapon, and since how he felt towards the weapon was part of the control, the weapon was made beautiful.

The M-1 rifle was somewhere between the two wars in

design, and looked and felt that way—something from late in the fourth archaeological period, when classic has given way to baroque and baroque begins to lack fine, carefully finished detail. I remember in training the noncommissioned creeps and idiots of cadre (when the commissioned ones weren't saying the same thing) telling us solemnly, over and over again, how deeply we would come to love our guns. The best moment in the army came when, being placed on detached service just after the war ended, I was allowed to turn my M-1 in to the supply room; I didn't have an instant of reluctant sentimentality about it, just felt tremendously tickled that I'd no longer have to carry, guard, or clean the damn thing.

(Comment, December, 1962—That was long ago, before I had ever seen a really stylish gun, before I'd ever been to Abercrombie and Fitch to see Boss and Purdy doubles, in all their wonderfully comfortable nineteenth-century elegance. I doubt I shall ever be able to afford one, but I do have a fine gun, now, from much lower on the fine-gun price scale—an over and under Beretta of good grade. It was a gift from my wife, and my pride in carrying it is an important realization of what began as a fantasy. It is not a weapon, really, but a piece of beautiful equipment, like fine luggage, a really good suit, or a custom saddle; a double gun is the walking man's yacht, the creation of a marvelous toymaker—until I mount it to my shoulder and shoot at something live. In the killing, even in the missing, fantasy ends. This is what I tried to tell Con Carter.)

Conversation with Con Carter, Spring 1961. While trout fishing.

(The trout weren't biting. We sat by a pool, and could see two small browns and a larger one, lying on the bottom. They had ignored our streamers. It was about ten in the morning, but we had got up very early and were eating lunch.)

Con said, "You liked bullfighting?"

"No, not at first. Then I liked it a lot for a while—hot and cold. We shared a house with an American girl bullfighter for a while, in Mexico City."

"What could she have been like?"

"Pretty."

"Good bullfighter?"

"Yes. But she could have been Manolete with curls and the fans still wouldn't have taken her for anything but a curiosity."

"I imagine."

"Actually, she had more guts than some of the men. Anyway, there were always bullfighters and managers and promoters and newspaper critics around the place. We got so ..."

"They have critics?"

"Yeah. We got so bullfighting was one of those things you hear about and experience incessantly and don't have that much real interest in."

"The old bellyful," Con said, and I saw that he was watching the fish. They weren't doing anything different as far as I could see, barely moving their tails in the current to stay in place. So I went on.

"Bullfighting's as dirty a racket as prize fighting, really. With a few special worse things about it. A lot of the critics and promoters are fags—and the horde of kids coming up, they're sort of tenderly virile young athletes. Like high-school football players, but hungrier. They come from little Indian villages, often enough, and there are the fat, perfumey, big shots waiting for them, who can do the favors."

"You don't think any of that goes on in prize fighting?"

I didn't know. "There's tampering with bulls," I said. "Kickbacks to get fights ... but when a kid gets in the ring, he does something brave. You can't alter that. You can shave a bull's horns, beat him over the kidneys till he's ready to drop, fill him with water to slow him down—but you can't get him to take a dive. He'll get you if he can, and it takes pure physical courage to face him. That's what the crowd pays to see, that and the ballet, the spectacle. And the killing."

"The old moment of truth?"

The larger trout suddenly left the pool, flashing away upsteam.

"That's the phrase."

"Why? Is that the most dangerous part for the fighter?"

[165]

Up at the head of the pool, the big trout began to feed near the surface. He broke water, not quite hard enough to splash, but we both saw it. Con was on his feet, grinning, tying on a dry fly, but I couldn't stop pontificating; it takes a moment to get a fly on.

"Not exactly. I didn't understand 'moment of truth' until I started hunting. Hunting's a play, sometimes, something like being a bullfighter without the danger, or the crowd. But—" Con was not really out of earshot, but I knew that the splash the fish made on his next rise, tiny as it was, drowned out anything I was saying to him. Probably I spoke to the two trout who were still lying at the bottom of the pool—"When you shoot, the fantasy ends. Death is always real. No matter what role you've been playing, death is the moment of truth, the moment when reality returns."

Should I fish upstream or down? Go to a dry fly? I finished my sandwich and a moment later Con came back with the trout. It took a moment for me to understand what he was asking:

"How about the girl? She like to kill those big male bulls?"

"Oh yes," I said. "Very much. It's always the males we want to kill, isn't it? Cock pheasants, buck deer ..."

"If I'm not mistaken, this is a male brown trout," Con said, grinning again and getting out his knife. "Let's open his stomach and see what sort of male bug he's been feeding on."

Excerpts: 1935, 1849, 1852. (How much that we learned from Hemingway there was in that conversation with Con—having recalled it, I look through *Green Hills,* and find Hemingway on killing):

"I did not mind killing anything, any animal, if I killed it cleanly, they all had to die and my interference with the nightly and the seasonal killing that went on all the time was very minute and I had no guilty feeling at all. We ate the meat and kept the hides and horns."

Thoreau, another of the stones I keep touching (in his *Week on the Concord and Merrimac Rivers):*

"We obtained one of these handsome birds [a passenger

pigeon] which lingered too long on its perch and broiled it here with some other game, to be carried along for our supper ... It is true it did not seem to be putting this bird to its right use to pluck off its feathers, and extract its entrails, and broil its carcass on the coals; but we heroically persevered, nevertheless, waiting for further information. The same regard for nature which excited our sympathies for her creatures nerved our hands to carry out what we had begun. For we would be honorable to the party we deserted; we would fulfill fate, and so at length, perhaps, detect the secret innocence of these incessant tragedies which heaven allows ... Nature herself has not provided the most graceful end for her creatures ... there is tragedy at the end of each of their lives. They must perish miserably.''

Pretty much the same thing that Hemingway says, more elaborately put—but, fellow Americans, why do we bring the matter up? Is it a peculiarly American (or American and British) thing to feel guilt, to have to rationalize the killing that accompanies sport, rather like the rationalizations we think of to justify drinking? To the one writer I refer to outside of our cultural pattern, Turgenev—a gentle, sympathetic man—the question that there may be guilt in a sportsman's killing can occur only in the mind of an addled and religious peasant eccentric whom he calls Kasyan from Fair Springs. Kasyan has asked to go along on the day's hunt, and Turgenev writes:

''For a long time I found no sport; at last, from a spreading oak-bush densely entwined with wormwood, a corncrake flew up. I hit him; he turned a somersault in the air and dropped...

'' 'Master, I say, master?' said Kasyan suddenly in his tuneful voice.

''I half-rose in surprise; hitherto he had hardly answered my questions and now he had suddenly addressed me himself.

'' 'What is it?' I asked.

'' 'Why did you kill that birdie?' he began, looking me straight in the face.

'' 'How do you mean, why? ... A corncrake is game; you can eat him.'

" 'That's not why you killed him, master, as if you were going to eat him! You killed him for your sport.'

"... I confess [says Turgenev, after listening to Kasyan explain the sin more thoroughly] that I looked at the strange old fellow in complete amazement.''

It does not occur to Turgenev that any noneccentric reader might have some objections to his killing—Turgenev's may be the "secret innocence" Thoreau wondered at. It would be the innocence, playfulness even, of an animal, however overdeveloped, who finds that it is in him to be excited and then satisfied by joining nature's natural killers, and makes a game of seeking that satisfaction. It is not Turgenev's innocence that seems to me secret, mystifying, but our guilt.

What was the question? Oh, okay: Peterson's *Field Guide* has it, in the Appendix dealing with *Accidentals:* "Corn Crake. *Crex crex.* At least fifteen records this side of the Atlantic, but only one or two in the past forty years. An upland field rail, of the short billed Sora type but larger; yellowish buff with conspicuous rufous-red wings."

Some comments on the excerpts, December 1962. For a time, referring first to Hemingway, I thought I might be able to manage a contempt for trophy hunting, making me a more elevated sort of sport. But to this, as to most notions of one's own superiority, the answer lies in a careful look at my own behavior. Am I so desperately fond of quail that I order them frozen, out of season, through the mail from quail raisers? Do we frequently buy frozen trout from the supermarket when the freezer at home is empty of the ones I caught? No, of course not. The care with which we dress and cook game, the time and expense to which I go to provide it for the table, indicate quite clearly that we serve and eat it as a trophy. There were five pheasants roasted and heaped up on a platter set before the guests at Christmas dinner, a day or two ago, and a dozen of the longest tail feathers were stuck upright into half an apple at the end.

As for squirrels, which Thoreau scorned ("we abandoned . . . as too wretched a resource for any but starving men . . . If they had been larger, our crime had been less . . .

mere gobbets of venison''), I find them very good. Rabbits, too. Yet I have less enthusiasm for hunting furred small game than I do for birds. If ever I tried to find some sort of Hindu significance in this, their blood and bodies being more like mine and so on, this too was exposed quite recently. Virgil Culross, who is an expert squirrel hunter, showed me a woodsmanlike way of stalking to get near them; I think I shall find, when squirrel season comes again next year, that my indifference has been the indifference of one who didn't really understand how to proceed. I shall have the same feeling, then, towards their lives that I have towards the lives of birds.

For I cannot claim to be, like Turgenev, guiltless. I have my share of the all-American, free-floating guilt which seems to feed on damn near anything we do for pleasure. My reaction insofar as it attaches itself to my shooting of other creatures, seems, however, to be not to rationalize but anaesthetize it. My precise feeling towards the individual bird or animal I have killed, once the excitement is past and the trophy eaten, is an absolute indifference, and I would claim, without feeling any sense of contradiction, that my feeling towards the same bird or animal, seen when I am not hunting it, is an almost perfect love.

The contradiction comes when I consider whether I am genuinely sensitive to the suffering of wounded game. This is the weakest point in the case I must make to myself—I am long past feeling that I must make a case for hunting to others. Again I watch my own behavior; again, I do not come out awfully well, for while I acknowledge that to be shot must hurt, and that it is an agony I cause, I must still suspect that the wretchedness I feel at wounding game and losing it proceeds as much from my loss, and from irritation with my own ineptness, as it does from real commiseration. This is callousness, and quite unlike the indifference I've described. It is a learned callousness, and I would date it from certain dressing stations, bombed towns, a ridge crossing . . . but I do not blame the war entirely. We grow up with more sensitivity than we can possibly use, and must, by the time we finish growing, have learned that you can never stop and think or it will break your heart.

This is black learning, of course, and may well be left to experience, which is a dark teacher. I will not begin to take my boy along hunting for as many years as may be. At five he is still too much a rabbit, a squirrel, and a winged bird himself for me to let him see me kill one. Yet it has begun: he likes to fish, and when he catches a small fish wants it kept alive, brought home. Larger fish he eats, with hunger and with pride. He has made me a cardboard target with various blobs on it and instructed me which I may shoot and which not—I may shoot lamprey, shark, and chicken blobs, but not the coon blob or the friendly crocodile.

Note, December 15, 1962 (The opening day of our three-day shotgun deer season). These are the three days I stay home, when the once-a-year boys are out with their shotguns loaded with heavy slugs. I should like a deer, should like to get one with a bow and arrow, or perhaps in another state where the season is long and leisurely and not frantic. But here? It is not many seasons since a sailor, hitchhiking through wooded parts and wearing whites to make himself as conspicuous as possible, found himself left along the highway. Hearing shots nearby he decided to be particularly careful, and climbed a tree. When the hunters dropped him, whites and all, he was thirty feet up and still climbing.

As I hunt, nothing much in the way of courage is involved. Even out of deer season someone might shoot me, I suppose, but a man takes his chances on fools in whatever he does in this world, and the fool on whom he takes the longest chance is the one towards whose grave he is heading. Other than men, there is nothing alive, waiting for me outdoors, that I need to fear. Snakes perhaps; yes, I'm afraid of them. But they are rare here, and of the things I actually hunt, not one could do me harm except a rabbit with tularemia, or the wrong kind of mushroom.

Cold could get me, I suppose. Or, as before, water.

December 3, 1962. From information requested by an income-tax auditor, substantiating a casualty of $350.00

Browning automatic, light 12, with vent polychoke, bought
spring 1959. Cost approx. $160.00. Fair market value $115.00
Zeiss monocular, bought spring 1959. Cost $90.00. Fair market
value 70.00
Camp stove and fuel 15.00
Blanket (2 @ $7.50) 15.00
Fishing lures and tackle box 20.00
10 boxes ammunition 35.00
Food (2 men, 7 days) 45.00
Jacket 20.00
Decoys 15.00

Was I speaking of fools and their graves? How many
lessons should even a fool need in the specific gravity of a pair
of hip boots full of water?

We were in the very middle of the lake. Studying the map
afterwards, we figured that we were something like three miles
out from the nearest point of shore—a huge, brown lake with
weeds and ducks way back, now, at the part we'd left. We had
five of the ducks with us, and all that gear I listed, and a good
deal more, too, like the tent, which floated; and things, come to
think of it, that I forgot to list—my good hunting knife, the big
flashlight. Some of the things on the list floated a little while,
like the blankets, but not for long enough; the duck decoys
were okay, of course. So were the bodies of the goose decoys,
but we lost all the heads.

Probably it was too much load for a small, aluminum duck
boat; probably we put too much of the weight towards the
bow. But we'd been going along without trouble, through
grey, quiet weather, for nearly an hour, when the wind came
up.

It was a sudden wind with a little rain in it, unexpectedly
forceful, quite brief in duration; a squall. Jerry had the
monocular to his eye, trying to pick out landmarks on the
blank shoreline we were moving towards, for a clue to where
we might have left the car. I cut the boat motor, so he'd have
less vibration—if the bow was going under, it should have
happened then. But it didn't, nor was there anything to suggest the possibility, and I restarted the old outboard, proud

[171]

of how well it was working, turning slightly to head towards an inlet Jerry had picked out. A large bunch of diving ducks, very high and strung out, went over us. When I looked down from them, I saw the squall coming along to meet us, turning the brown water black; felt the rain first and wondered if we were going to be cold. A little water splashed in over the bow, but that was always happening. I hoped we hadn't put the bread up there.

We bobbed up just a little; we bobbed down, and then, slowly, unbroken as the flow over the lip of a dam, water poured quietly in all along the front edge of our square bow, barely an inch of it but without stopping. Jerry, still half-turned and looking at the shoreline from the middle seat, saw it when I did, turned back towards me, and said with mysterious dignity:

"Look. We're in trouble."

He pushed back towards me away from the center seat, unable to disengage his legs from the duffel and boxes on the floor between us, trying to get his own weight away from the bow. It raised the bow slightly, but not enough. The pouring continued, leisurely, unstoppable.

I remember how my panic felt; it was a sensation of physical stoppage, both breathless and bloodless, as if my heart had stopped and, like any pump, was pulling the blood back from all over my body towards the vacuum. I think I said, "Yes, yes," and I know that I started undoing the motor in the seconds when the water level was rising gradually in the bottom of the boat, coming up first over my toes, then over my ankles. One or two decoys began to float in front of me near the floor, and it was then, fumbling still with the motor, that I saw, coldly, so absolutely frightened that my fear could not increase, that I was still wearing hip boots. We'd been unable to use the motor, coming away through weeds; I'd kept my boots on so that I could wade and push, and when I climbed into the boat, I hadn't wanted to trouble with changing to shoes.

Jerry and I went out at the same time, over the same side, while the boat was still half full. I remember that I'd begun to breathe again, in gasps, past the fear in my throat, as

I pushed into the lake, went down as far as my waist bracing against the edge of the boat, and saw the shoreline far away in the rain. Jerry had the edge, too, right next to me, and we were pushing together down on it, without consultation, trying to turn it over so that the gear would dump out, the bottom come up, and the flotation foam, in blocks under the seats, have a chance to function. We couldn't turn it.

It kept going down, under our hands, and I looked at Jerry's white face, envied his free legs, and let go. My hands went to my belt, and I drew my legs up as well as I could hoping to get rid of pants, boots and all, but doubting that I could. And suddenly I heard strange, wet, choking laughter; I turned my face, and there was Jerry, standing up, shoulders clear; big as it was, the lake was only five feet deep, and I stretched my toes towards the benevolent mud.

Final note, before the final entry. End of the year 1962. December 31. Unable to deal directly with the question of death, I have tried to surround it, writing of the deaths of birds, of my own close calls. There is a gap in the encirclement, an open arc, and with this last entry I shall try to close it. It was written earlier this year, within a few days after the event. From the look of things so far, we are about to have another winter like it:

This is Old Branch, Iowa (I wrote), the 10th of February, 1962, where we are having a hard winter, just as you are.

Last night, when I was helping put the children to bed, the fire siren began to howl. It was so cold that we had brought our beagle in from the kennel and put her in the cellar; the kennel is heated but part of my response to the weather is to want everything dependent on me under a single roof. Now the dog in the basement began to howl along with the siren.

Every man living in this town of eight houses belongs, by assumption, to the Volunteer Fire Department. I put the little boy I had been carrying around down on his bed, and said to his mother:

"It's a hell of a night for a fire." The thermometer was at four degrees below zero, too cold to snow, but it was snow-ing anyway, slightly and steadily.

I still had on insulated boots and insulated underwear which I had worn in the afternoon for a drive into town; there, while I did some things at my office, our older child, a daughter, had taken her regular piano lesson and afterwards been fitted with ice skates, a reward for the cold she suffered on the drive. They do not make the insulated garments in children's sizes.

Over my own I now put on a short, sheepskin-lined coat; I turned up the collar, put on heavy deerskin mittens, and an alpaca-lined hat, tying the ear flaps down with a ribbon which goes under my chin. It's a rather funny-looking hat, worn that way, but there is a point on the thermometer which might be marked *vanity;* the temperature was certainly subvanity. I trotted out to the garage, feeling no sensation of cold except when the wind touched my face. I was pleased that the clothes had been ready, for I'd been unprepared for, and then late to, the last winter-night fire. That was six weeks ago. Some friends and I were drinking and playing music in the basement and didn't hear the siren. By the time my wife could make me understand what was going on outdoors, and I was dressed and ready, it was too late to follow the fire truck as I usually do. I have not lived in the community all my life, and do not automatically know whose farm is where; I'd had to stop to ask directions twice.

Now, hurrying, I tried to drive the car out without warming it up, assuming it would still have heat left in the block from the trip to town; it didn't. It stalled, and when I got it going again, I sat there impatiently racing the engine, imagining the fire truck going off again without my seeing where.

I needn't have worried. The truck was still inside when I got to the firehouse, three blocks away; the door hadn't even been opened and I could see the red of the truck behind the glass of the window, through frost.

Bern Cilek, the fire chief who is also bartender and lessee at one of the two local taverns, was in front of the door. He is a slight, high-strung man, and makes a good chief. I put down the window of the car and Bern called to ask if I had a flashlight with me.

"I can get one from home in a minute," I said.

"You'll need it," Bern called, and then, coming a step nearer the car, "There's a man dead out in the timber. We're going to look for him."

When I got back with the light, Bern was still there, directing cars. He told a boy standing by to ride with me. I asked if the boy knew where to go, and Bern said:

"It's on the road to the lake. Just go out along it till you see the cars."

We drove off through the falling snow along the secondary highway which I use daily to go to the University; the flakes were tiny, fine as rain and falling slantwise across the beam of the headlight. The boy was wearing one of the rubber jackets which hang in the firehouse, and an unlined hat; he said he didn't expect to be cold, but I imagined a long night walking through the woods, looking for the dead man. I had thought of bringing Moon when I went back for the light, and decided not to; his feet would freeze on a night like this.

"How do they know about the man in the woods?" I asked.

"It's Dan Bunning," the boy said. "At least I guess it is."

"Fox-hunting?"

"Yes. He didn't get back. That's what I heard someone say."

"Do they know he's dead? How would anybody know?"

"I just said what I heard at the firehouse."

"If it was Dan," I said, "and he was wearing those snowshoes, we may be going a long way into the woods."

I thought about Dan Bunning's snowshoes. They are the only ones I know of in this locality; ordinarily the snow which falls in a winter melts off every second or third week. This winter the ground has been covered since before Christmas. I am out in it, most days, exercising the dogs; there is about ten inches in the average place, with a two-inch crust, and over it whatever cover of new snow has fallen recently. The crust is not quite strong enough to support my weight, and the few hundred yards I go with the dogs, breaking through crust and lifting each foot out again, are enough to exhaust me, though

I am quite used to walking. Snowshoes have been in my mind more than once. Dan used to say last summer, when I would take my car to the local garage for him to fix, and would notice his shoes hanging high on the wall, that it was a surprise to him how easy they are to use. "We may be going a long way into the woods, if it's Dan," I said again, meaning: a long, hard way.

But then we never got into the woods at all. We got only as far as a farm, where the firemen were gathering, their flashlights and headlights reflecting off banked snow, picking up fences, trees, the farmhouse, at random angles, and making the dark look darker.

Dan Bunning's brother Tarve was one of them. One sees Tarve at the garage, too, working with his brother; the garage is one of seven retail businesses in Old Branch. The others are a filling station, two groceries, the grain-and-feed company, and the two taverns. The taverns exist not on local patronage but as roadhouses, drawing their customers from the university town, and outside the jurisdiction of its police. The only other money I can think of coming into town is the two-man payroll at the post-office. There are a few self-employed: an electrician, a plumber, a trucker; there are the schoolteachers, but none of them lives here; there is a man who writes insurance for the farmers near Old Branch. All the rest of us are supported from outside, and mostly we go either eight miles in one direction or seventeen in the other to our work. This includes probably sixty of the eighty households, and makes Dan Bunning a key man in Old Branch. It is essential to the town's life that the cars run, and on these bitter mornings the towtruck from the garage can be seen moving through the streets as urgently as might a doctor's car during an epidemic.

I always found Dan a pleasant man, though not everyone did. I remember the only time I had any cause to discuss him, outside of my family; a very old man and wife called on us, just before the last town elections. They were supporting a slate on which Dan and some others were running against the incumbents; this was not a reform slate—the incumbents had been. Dan's slate was for a return to conservative local policy,

[176]

for things as they were and taxes low.

"Some think Dan Bunning's kind of strong in his opinions and argumentative," the old man had said. It was news to me. I never saw that side of Dan; the one time I heard him declaim on a local issue, what he'd said made sense; and if there was a taint of New England-like self-esteem in the certainty with which his opinions were stated, I'd found it not inappropriate in a man who worked as hard, as well, and as reasonably as Dan did. A nice-looking man, forty to forty-five; a bachelor. These were the things I found myself thinking as we got out of the car at the farm past which he (or someone else) had gone into the woods to die.

Seeing Tarve, his brother, there, more or less taking charge, convinced me it was Dan, for Tarve is not an assertive man ordinarily. But it was he whom the other men looked to for direction; it was he who seemed to know what had happened.

"He's down there," Tarve said, when I greeted him, and since he assumed I knew whom he meant, I could not ask, *Is it really Dan?* It is not so much that I had doubts, rather that news of death is something which cannot be accepted until authority is clear and absolute.

"They called him up this afternoon to say there was a couple of fox," Tarve said, and "they" must mean the people at this farm. "They saw them go into a hole, down in the timber."

That seemed to be enough for the boy who had ridden out with me, for he got back into my car, now, for warmth, since nothing was happening to involve him, and indeed it did pretty well complete the evidence. For Dan and Tarve are our only fox hunters, as far as I know. Fox hunting is a pursuit which takes a particular combination of temperament, physique, and experience which would not be likely to occur in more than one of eighty households. It takes stamina and strong legs to begin with; I doubt that they have ever heard of hunting foxes from horseback in this tractor and barbed-wire part of the country. They go out on foot, not with a pack but with a single dog, and snow time is the time for it for two reasons: a running fox shows up against the snow, hundreds of yards away if you know how to look for it; and when you get to the spot, there are tracks to follow. Then you must plot which way you judge the dog and fox will move, and get yourself to a place where you are likely to have a shot; or you may call in the dog, and track and stalk the fox, with the dog at heel, in perfect silence. A man on foot does not run a fox down, and what he does do is only slightly less unlikely: he intercepts or steals up on the animal.

Besides Dan and Tarve Bunning, I've known only one real fox hunter, an old man of the woods down south of town who hunts them for bounty and the price of skins—small matters, with a two-dollar bounty and a poor fur market, but enough to make the difference between tobacco and no tobacco when one lives on a pension check. Dan, of course, did not hunt for the bounties; he hunted for the sake of hunting foxes, and he hunted nothing else. He had no interest in ducks or quail or pheasants; he was one of those, I suppose, who need in hunting a sense not merely of quarry but of adversary, and I suppose further that it is this need (for myself, I do not feel it) which makes big-game hunters.

Tarve said that a four-wheel drive pick-up truck had gone into the woods, following a tractor with heavy chains which preceded it to make a path, and that we were waiting now to see whether they could succeed in reaching the body without our going in. I learned, too, why there was a general presumption of death.

"He had a heart attack three years ago," Tarve said. "He was supposed to carry some pills and take them whenever he got dizzy. But it looks like he didn't take them in time."

It was two below zero in the woods yesterday afternoon, and one does not wear, for hunting, such heavy clothes as I had on. A light stroke, which would cause nothing worse than a few hours' pain and discomfort in the living room, followed by a lot of anxiety, will kill a man outdoors in this winter's temperatures; the stroke, like a wound from an inaccurate shot, stops the victim, and winter does the rest.

This is our second winter fatality in Old Branch this bitter season; the first was a man of fifty, whose house is only four away from ours. My daughter sometimes short-cuts through the yard of that house, on her way to school. He was caught out in his car, in one of the storms, late at night; went off the road and could not keep warm enough as he waited for help. That could happen anywhere, couldn't it?

From the woods we saw headlights returning, and there was a murmur of men who did not know asking other men who had no way of knowing, "Do they have him?" There may have been twenty of us, stamping snow and asking each other. I walked with Tarve Bunning sixty yards or so to open a gate, and as we went, the headlights of the two vehicles, the truck and the tractor, came pitching slowly towards us across the whiteness.

They had him. I'm not quite sure how we knew it, as we stood at the gate and they went past, for we could not see into the truck body, and neither of the two men riding in it looked at us or said a word. It must have been the stillness of their faces that told us. The tractor was coming more slowly, half a field behind, as we turned to follow the truck.

And still I was only certain it was someone dead, almost surely Dan, but Tarve hadn't said his name. So I crowded in with the others, around the back of the pick-up, too much at the edge of the circle to offer to help unload, but profoundly curious to see.

An ambulance had come. A stretcher from it was placed on the ground. When the body was lifted down, so stiff it took only two men holding at the waist, I could see the top of a head, a forehead, and the upper rim of glasses. I did not see the face; I still could not have turned to anyone and assured him, "Yes. It's Dan all right."

A doctor was there. He knelt over the body, blankets were placed on it, and several men lifted the stretcher into the ambulance.

Then there were several things said, of the kind that come with a release of tension:

"He's gone, boy."

"Done kicked the bucket."

"Old Dan's hunted his last fox."

There was the name, attached to the fact, and at last I was

[179]

altogether sure; so I thought of Dan's last fox. It had been lying on the floor of the garage, last time I took my car in there, a delicate red animal, smaller than one remembers, with its ears stiffly perked, its color rich against the oily concrete floor, a little blood around its open mouth, and teeth like knife points. It was frozen; it was being allowed to thaw so that it might be skinned. I remember a coon someone gave me once which was frozen that way; it was almost two days before it was pliant enough to work on.

Tarve said: "I want to thank you all for coming out"; and, since we were standing together; since our daughters play together and his older girl sometimes sits with our children; since he asked me once to vote for Dan, and since we have agreed that we will hunt together sometime (though I do not know that we really will), I felt I knew him just a shade too well to say nothing, but I had no idea what to say.

"I'm very sorry," or something like that, is what I muttered, to which Tarve replied:

"Thank you for coming out in this weather."

I drove home alone. The boy who'd ridden with me got a ride with friends. And when I walked into the house, I had not yet been gone long enough for the activity they'd been engaged in to have changed. The little boy was asleep, but his sister was still being read to. My wife called downstairs to ask where the fire had been, and if it was over already, and I called up:

"It's all right. No fire."

My daughter is interested in the fires I go to, and I generally describe them for her; but I thought it better, last night, to wait until her mother came downstairs. I didn't want the child left to go to sleep in the winter night with the news I brought the last thing in her mind.

Mr. Levine: We have put our Unnatural Enemy through a good many mishaps and frustrations. Now at last I think we are ready to let him succeed in killing a bird; shall it be a duck?

There is an old print I've always liked, a woodcut from England I think, called "Death and the Falconer." I used to see it in the print collection at the New York Public Library, if I'm not mistaken.

It shows the Falconer as a young buck, with bird on wrist, confronted by a medieval representation of death as a grinning skeleton—scythe, hour glass, and all that equipment people imagined him using to hunt with. The Falconer is attempting to grin back at death, but can't quite make it—his grin is a simper. He looks quite idiotic.

The falcon looks indifferent.

I think our Unnatural Enemy, rather a middle-aged buck, or I (or perhaps you), would look pretty idiotic too, confronted by death in the form of a skeleton. And of course the confrontation, without a form, is always implied when we hunt and always exposed when we kill.

Could you draw, to close the book, The Unnatural Enemy (or me; or perhaps you) and his dead bird, with something of this in mind?

Leave the dog out, I think. Moon could never stand for an indifferent falcon.

If you want to be fancy you could even curve the dead duck's bill a little, to give an almost imperceptible suggestion of the scythe.

NEW ACQUAINTANCE